Giving Up the Ghost
(and other Hauntings)

Giving Up the Ghost
(and other Hauntings)

Tina V. Cabrera

atmosphere press

TABLE OF CONTENTS

What Happens to Me...

DAY OF NO DEAD

My habit of obsessing over matters large and small only intensified after learning of my sister's cancer diagnosis in 2013. We were driving to Kansas to celebrate Thanksgiving with my husband's family when I got the news. I threw my phone, an action that felt ineffectual and fraudulent. I don't remember the minor details, such as how the news was delivered, whether by phone call or text, or what happened immediately after; did we talk about anything else for the remainder of the road trip? Did we continue to listen to music, or did we sit in silence?

Dyna died of stage IV lung cancer just three months later, on February 13, 2014. Being the day before Valentine's Day makes the anniversary of her death easier to remember. My husband and I regularly celebrate the holiday by going out for a special dinner. Despite Dyna's death the day before, this Valentine's was no exception. Dyna died during the spring semester, while I was taking "The Personal Essay," a required class for the Creative Nonfiction PhD program at the University of North Texas. Unsurprisingly, my writing in this class revolved around themes of loss; just a couple of weeks prior to her death, the first personal essay I wrote for workshop in part explored our strained relationship, and the second one was an early draft of this one I am revising right now. The former's concern was with coping with loss, and the latter's primarily the human need to pay homage to the memories of loved ones through the ritual of obituary writing. My professor used the word "monstrous" to describe my juxtaposing the loss of treasured objects—

such as a pair of expensive sunglasses and my favorite pen—with the loss of my sibling. I stayed silent during the workshopping of my piece, as is common practice for creative writing workshops, but felt my face flush from shame at the revelation, for I had not even realized the comparison. I started writing that essay the previous semester when I had experienced three losses within three months: my 8-year old cat had died from cancer, my other cat ran away during an ice storm, and Dyna was diagnosed with lung cancer. *Is it vulgar to feel more grief over the loss of a pet than the impending death of a family member, no matter the nature of that relationship?*

The eulogy for my sister was divided into three chapters and traces the major events and turning points in her life: born in Yokosuka, Japan; grew up in San Diego, California; baptized as a Jehovah's Witness at age 13; married her best friend at 18. It praises her as having been a most outstanding mother and wife, always reliable when it came to her family. Those closest to her say her strong faith remained intact until the last minutes of her life. I don't know who wrote the memorial tribute, whether it was my brother-in-law alone, my nephew, niece, or all three collaboratively. And at once this discomforting thought occurs to me: *How do they know that her faith truly remained unwavering? What if she doubted in those last minutes of her life?*

When someone dies, someone else is usually authorized to encapsulate his or her life. The job of the eulogy or obituary writer is to summarize the deceased's life succinctly, resisting the urge to fill in the blanks with could-bes or maybes. *Could it be she doubted her God at the very end? The God who allowed her to suffer while saving others from misery? Could it be she sometimes faltered from being the perfect wife and mother? Maybe she longed to fulfill herself in other ways besides devoting herself to the needs of others?* But speculation is irrelevant and arranging the loved one's past like photos in a family album is meant to bring the mourners closer to closure.

We must move on, but before we do, pay tribute to the dead out of love and respect. Yet - how does one go about summarizing a life?

Obituaries are supposed to do just that. The Internet and other sources proliferate with instructions on how to write an obituary. The most basic format asks you to state the deceased's entire name and date of death, followed by family background, marriage(s), life passions, education, achievements and awards.

Beyond the basics, you have what funeral homes call *exceptional* obituaries (meaning the deceased lived a rich, interesting life). You may include all or most of the following:

- The deceased's entire name.

- The deceased's death information (date, location, cause, age at death, and a personal comment such as "surrounded by family" or "comforted by her husband"). NB: Sometimes it is desirable to omit the cause of death, such as when death came as a result of extreme violence or the carrying out of a court sentence. Only when the person died a so-called "natural" death is it deemed appropriate to mention the cause: *Betty died peacefully in her sleep.* How do we know? Doesn't this kind of jargon assume that sleep is a universally tranquil experience? Ever struggle in the grips of a nightmare that's anything but peaceful? Of course, the following version of Betty's obituary is not likely to make it into any paper: *Betty died some time during the hours of sleep. We know this because it was determined by the coroner's office. We aren't certain whether she struggled against death in the last moments because – well – we weren't there, and she overdosed on prescribed barbiturates and sleeping pills. Accidental or purposeful? The point is moot. What matters is that Betty was alive and now she is dead. We will never know whether she died peacefully (whatever that means) or fought bravely to stay alive or to die, or something or nothing in between.*

- The deceased's birth information.

- A brief story of the deceased's life, in loose, chronological order, including relatives who preceded the deceased in death, who the deceased is survived by, the memorial and gravesite, special thanks (to whom or what for is up to the author's discretion), and finally where to send condolences. It may not be wise to list a material address. Besides, most transactions in sentiment are now electronic.

As you can see, the task can appear daunting. Although the space allocated for obituaries varies, both in print and online newspapers, most funeral homes and sites that offer instructions on how to write obituaries recommend keeping them brief.

Some examples of brief obituaries on record for public viewing demonstrate existent efforts on the part of writers to write with conciseness and brevity.

Notice how much you can pack in only one or two

lines:

FRANCO, JULIAN Predeceased by wife and now they are together in heaven.

DURAN, DINA Chef extraordinaire, devoted god-mother of Lizzy, loving cousin to Fred.

RHYDE, RONALD Left us on July 11 at 0815. Passed away in the company of a visiting troop of showgirls.

LIN, LEE Born in Los Angeles, California, the land of opportunity. Died somewhere else.

Some lives could be summarized like lines on a tombstone:

JOHNSON, JOHN G. Born July 1, 1952. Died May 1, 2003. John wrote books. He died.

Or like lines of poetry:

KOVAN, GER Mother of two, friend of dozens.

LIZARRO, CASS Loved her family. Loved the Lord.

Obits like this give you pause:

MARCUS, LEANN Lived a full life, demonstrated in part by her loyal dedication to the firm for 30 years.

How about ones that would do well as "Today I Feel" magnets displayed on the refrigerator:

ALVAREZ, EDWARD Surgeon at Sharp Medical for 40 years. Died two years after retirement.

SOMMERS, BARB Experimented with new forms of plastic surgery. Luckily, died before ever needing any.

CALLIS, DIMITRI Wrote Y.A. novels. Married 20 years. Left behind a wife but no children.

BACKER, BECKA Author of children's books. Died without ever having any.

TATE, RONALD FAYE 01/24/36 – 10/7/2015 Preferred Cremation & Burial.

VALANZUELA, MANUEL "MANNY" ZEPEDA Preferred to dig his own grave.

The thing about writing an obituary is that you must search through memories (yours or someone else's) for moments, and amidst those moments, patterns. You hope to see lives come together in meaningful shapes: *Baptized at the young age of 13, she must have loved her God so much. Marrying her best friend, she loved him for his mind and heart. Though married young, she remained so to the same person all her life. If her faith faltered, it wasn't apparent. She never said so.* You seek the way a researcher does to puzzle the pieces together so that, somehow, they stick, they cohere. You hope to prove a life.

My sister and I were not close. Perhaps that is why I was not asked to write or contribute to her memorial. But I remember. Without effort, memories will return, not the big events in her life such as her baptism or wedding. I remember more recent things, like how she lay in the hospital bed, her left leg trembling. The shock I felt at seeing her head nearly bald when just two weeks prior her full hair had been pulled back in a long ponytail. Bending over to kiss her cheek and seeing dismembered stands of hair strewn on the pillow. Her eyes closed. My brother placing a mask with fake eyes over her face and trying to neither smile nor weep.

Memories from long ago return, too: My sister yelling at me for the relentless squeaking of the hamster wheel in the middle of the night. I found Tinkerbell dead not long after.

When my sister died, we hadn't seen each other in three years, and hardly spoke on the phone. Our lives were distant because she remained a Jehovah's Witness. Because of our age difference. Because. Without truly knowing my sister, I didn't have the right to write her tribute. Still, she was my sister. I try to fill in the gaps, offer explanations, if only in my mind. I speculate.

Jehovah's Witnesses believe that one day, "death will be no more." Though I don't believe this, the scriptural phrase lingers in my head. I imagine what it would be like if in the future—for just one day—no one were to die. This would result in no one having to summarize the life of someone who has passed that day because no one will pass. To put it more plainly, no one would have to bother even attempting to summarize the lives of those who otherwise died. What, then would take the place of efforts at encapsulation?

There are two sisters. They are close. Rather than one sister envisioning herself at the other's funeral and what she ought to say in her live eulogy, the sisters will most likely do things with each other on this day of no dead. Because both sisters will still be working things out in their lives, they will have options.

They will most likely a) go to the movies; b) go shopping c) go out to dinner. These three choices primarily correlate with the older sister's interests, and the younger will agree to them because she is passive and agreeable; however, the younger sister usually goes to movies alone.

Though recently, she had a souring experience on a visit to an independent theater so that she may not continue going to the movies alone. Besides this, her family and friends, one of whom may write an obituary about her life in the future are most likely not aware of her private life, for more often than not, she doesn't tell anyone about it; she's afraid of being seen as a strange loner going to the movies solo.

The thing is, after this one day of no dead, things will go back to normal; people will go back to dying every day, so that we can say with absolute certainty something that we always have been able to say—that one day in the future both siblings will die. It is likely that when one sister dies, if the other is still alive, she will write the obituary for her sister, and vice-versa. Because of their relationship, both sisters will obsess over how to summarize her sibling's life in less than 100 words. The sisters will have to omit many things.

If the older sister dies at a young age, the younger will certainly weep, but she will also speculate on whether she too, will die a young death. Of course, she won't include this in the obituary that permits only the most general summary sprinkled with touches of light. Even though she could justify including this fear if she really wanted to, the younger sister will not do so out of respect for the constraints built into obituary writing, even though she feels strongly that this fact, this worry is so closely linked to her sister.

If the older sister dies, the younger will feel guilt for not telling her about her lone visits to the movies and will be tempted to include this guilt in the obituary, which of course she won't; after all, the obituary is not about her. She will feel guilty for sticking to the script: [Enter name] enjoyed regularly going to the movies without her sister, her closest friend.

Somehow, I have strayed from my speculation on what would take the place of summarizing the lives of those who have died. Because this is a day of no dead, the sisters will not worry about compartmentalizing each other. They will do what they do.

On this day, they will not do as Doris Lessing does in her innovative memoir *Alfred & Emily,* which consists of two parts: the first, an imagined life for her parents and their relationship had World War I not taken place, and the second an attempt to articulate the same subject, only this time as it really was. In the nonfiction part, Lessing attempts to sum up her father in brief sentences, only to draw the conclusion that her "sentence resume" does not do him justice. In the last sentence of this section and of the novella, Lessing sums her mother up in this way: "She was, they all said, a very good bridge player."

Why—besides paying tribute—do we seek to summarize a life or sanction the writing of a life summary in the first place? I think part of it is related to a particular kind of fear.

Jorge Luis Borges, in his articulation of "Blindness," quotes a sentence by Rudolph Steiner that comes from his theosophy, "that when something ends, we must think that something begins." Borges then surmises that "the execution is difficult, for we only know what we have lost, not what we will gain. We have a very precise image—an image at times shameless—of what we have lost, but we are ignorant of what may follow or replace it."

In Borges's case, when he went blind, what he lost was "the beloved world of appearances" so that he felt obliged to "create something else." When someone close to us dies, we lose a relationship and must create one in its place. We may possess images of the very thing (person) we have lost, even one vast image that without words represents the immensity of that gap. We fear being swallowed up by the profoundness, especially if we lose someone that we loved deeply. The loss is one that we wish to articulate within a contained space because if we fail to do so, the enormity threatens to equal the enormity of the future. If we can sum up a person's life, we can reassure ourselves that we knew them and what they meant. Likewise, when we can at least pin down what begins when something ends, then we can attribute meaning to this new start.

Doris Lessing says that she wrote about her father "in various ways; in pieces long and short, and in novels... One may write a life in five volumes, or in a sentence. How about this? Alfred Tayler, a vigorous and healthy man was wounded badly in the First World War, tried to live as if he were not incapacitated, illnesses defeated him, and at the end of a shortened life he was begging, 'You put a sick old dog out of its misery, why not me?'" For Lessing, this "sentence ignores impressive things."

Obituaries and memories intend. Obituaries aspire to pay homage to the life of the deceased, and so paint the picture complete while leaving out the vague. Memories intend to reconstruct the past whether they ought to or not. Like us, they are fuzzy about certainties.

But we keep reading and writing obituaries, even though they fail to fully satisfy. Even though they necessarily ignore vast reservoirs of memory. So, we continue to pick and choose which memories to include, resigned to the knowledge that no book or bank of memories can contain all that one has lived. Even if they could, they are not capable of recording what we don't see.

13

DREAM REALITY

If—as some believe—we create and consume stories to try on variations of the Self, and if stories inform our dreams, then dream-selves are just as (un)real as the lives we call reality.

Last night's dream: My dead sister attended a wedding with my living sister and me.

While in the waking world, she was a bottle-blond and dressed modestly, but in the dream, she wore a fancy black and white silk dress, her skin was sun-tanned, and her hair was pitch black.

Dream living sister sported a man's tuxedo and walked with an imposing gait. (Waking world sister dresses in skirts and heels and though not entirely modest, does not walk with brazen conceit.)

After she died, my nephew told me that his mother always said she was ugly, and I wasn't surprised. I remember the hesitance with which she often carried herself, the opposite of dream living sister whose waking world counterpart often enters a room with self-confidence and pride. The living sister I know in this (un)reality would not be caught wearing men's clothing, yet I recognized her dream-self through the hazy figment of dream memory.

*

If dream narratives seem muddled and vague, maybe the fault lies not with dreams, but with dream memory. Maybe dream stories are rich and vibrant with detail, plot, and logic, but we cannot remember with this reality's sharpness. Dreams are like music—you cannot explain what it is about the melody that moves you or draws you in. Like music, dreams are impressionistic. Dreams are not the stuff of science or the intellect. Not any better or worse than waking reality, just different.

*

My sister is dead. She died a terrible death. I heard more in her voice over the phone than I ever did in person. She spoke with an altered voice—scratchy and soft. Rather than speak, she sobbed and I—unsure how to comfort—could only falsely reassure: "Oh, it's going to be okay." From more than a thousand miles away, I could hear the death rattle even before it began.

I can see her now, though she died three years ago—vacant eyes, a shell of a human being. She is with me yet. I can't forget: the sterile floor, shuffling down the cold corridor with the guidance of Papa's elbow. Like Mama's death, all-enveloping yet lingering. That evasion of the eyes. Why? My sister died before she died. The body yet moves with little vigor left, mechanically, from auto-memory, like a chicken without its head. A terrible death. Every death is terrible, I guess, unless you die in your sleep.

I thought of her from time to time, when we lived far apart. Sometimes it would be a childhood memory, sometimes imaginary scenes. The same thing happens now that she's dead. And in dreams. A reality my mind projects. Phenomena of the mind.

Scientists claim that our consciousness lags reality by seconds; if it takes some seconds for our senses to catch up, then is this dog lying next to me on the couch really here right now, or is her presence a mere after-image? Can I ever catch up to the world "out there"?

Dream is even more delayed than waking reality; its after-effects hit me hours after I wake up. For dream reality, that equates to infinity. Perhaps that is why dream narratives are vague and hazy, easily forgotten, difficult to remember. Too much time passes by in between. By the time I remember elements of my dream, the dream has altered, so that I am left with vague impressions. When I try to re-tell a dream, much is lost in translation.

*

Sleep and dreams are like death. I would guess. I would prefer the dulled sensations of vague dreams over the harsh upsets of my waking days.

*

Do I recognize my dead sister only in the remembering of the dream or when dreaming? There must be dream logic. Maybe dream is the dumping ground of memory. Dreams' attempts at narrative are like the work of a mad genius. Dream dead sister directed an illogical script, and I sensed our unease. Dream selves take backstage to persona, to aura. She is still my sister, even in costume, masked in dream body and skin.

ONE PHOTO OF MIGUEL CECILIO

1979

I met Grandpapa in a photo: Bushy eyebrows, full lips, wavy hair cropped close to the head. Dressed in a wool suit jacket worn over a white dress shirt, bow tie with a crosshatched design. He was a young man in the photo, and I was ten.

Three-quarter face photo in sepia, crookedly cropped and set in a 12 x 18-inch frame. Indiscriminately written on the back of the photo in blue ink cursive, *Miguel Cecilio,* and the year 1938.

Grandpapa Miguel Cecilio's moustache, a small patch above his lip, resembled Hitler's. And yet he looked more like a poet asking the camera to linger long. His eyes.

Mama told me she was born in 1941, though her birth certificate says she was born in 1940. Whether the truth is the former or the latter, the point is that this photo of Grandpa must have been taken only two or three years before Mama was born. Mama said he died when she was three. He looks no more than 30 in the photo, which means he became a father and died at a relatively young age.

Papa says that Filipinos tend to date their photos arbitrarily, meaning they'll often pick up a photo taken from who knows when, and write the date or year that they look at the photo, as if truly seeing it for the first time. So, then no one knows for sure if this photo of Grandpapa was really taken in 1938. Maybe Grandmama (assuming she's the one most likely to have labeled the photo) decided

17

to date it on the day Grandpapa gave it to her, rather than writing down the year it was taken. Or, if Grandpapa didn't give it to her, perhaps the photo slipped out of the pages of a magazine, cookbook, or out of Grandpapa's private diary only to be discovered accidentally. Perhaps Grandmama found it stuck between the cushions of his favorite armchair, or underneath the kitchen sink. No one knows for sure, but what this means is that there's the possibility this photo was taken years *before* 1938—say as early as 1930 or even 1928. If this is the case, then this man who would become my grandfather became father to my mother at an older age than imagined previously, which would mean that he *didn't* die all that young after all.

Whatever the case, what is known for certain is that the man in the photo left behind a wife and son in Spain and sometime later married a woman in the Philippines, the young woman named Lourdes who became my grandmother, who was a mere teenager at the time. They had two daughters together.

Only one photo remains of Grandpapa Miguel Cecilio: an up-close profile of his face with a moustache and brown eyes. He appears young in the photo, and by any standard, a handsome man.

1944 (or 43)

Grandmama told her two daughters—Josephine, the woman who became my mother and Patricia, the woman who became my aunt—that their father had been killed by a wild boar while hunting, that he bled to death after being gored. Apparently, this happened when my mother was three years old.

Adult male wild boars develop tusks that serve as tools and weapons. Adult female boars also have sharp canines, but they do not protrude like the male's.

Wild boars forage in the early morning hours or late afternoon. The male lowers its head, charges, and then slashes upward with his tusks. The female—whose tusks are not visible—charges with her head up, mouth wide, and bites. Such attacks are not often fatal to humans, but may result in severe trauma, dismemberment, or blood loss.

Miguel Cecilio did not lose a limb. A female boar—in an effort to protect her young—might have charged him. He did not stop to observe whether the boar attacked from a solitary position or from a sounder.

It isn't important to know whether the boar that gored Miguel Cecilio was male or female. Either way, an attack could lead to blood loss, which could lead to one bleeding to death. The story goes that Miguel Cecilio bled to death from a fatal wound, whether a bite or a slash. Such attacks are not usually fatal to humans.

1980

By the time Mama reached midlife, she had had six children. I, the youngest of four girls, one day inquired about Grandfather Miguel Cecilio. "Call him Grandpapa Miguel Cecilio," she said, "even though you never met him." I told my classmates the story you told me, I said to Mama. My friends giggled and ask me to tell the story again and again. Had Grandpapa really been killed by a wild boar? At last, Mama told me, the story goes that he really died of a fatal illness, most likely cancer, one of the real leading causes of death. I was disappointed. I preferred the heroic tale over and above this ordinary one. But if it's just a story, I asked, then how do you know it's true? She said she didn't know for certain, and that this was a story in circulation, among relatives and family members that made its way from the Philippines.

Grandpapa only knew his daughter—the woman who became my mother—until the age of three. He never knew that she would die of a rare cancer at the age of 58.

Only five percent of women who get uterine cancer get this most deadly kind. This is what the doctor told us. Because of this stark statistic, I remember the doctor's name. "There's no way of explaining it," Dr. Schumann said. "It's a proven medical fact." He told us the cancer had spread to her lymph nodes, as we hovered over his desk, Mama absent, sleeping from the operation that emptied her of her uterus and ovaries. She did not speak of it, at least not to me, not openly. Not until she knew she was really dying. "Why me?", she said. And I created a story to explain it, inside my head.

Mama's uterus had been overworked, giving birth to six of us children. She and Papa never used birth control. It wasn't something they talked about – at least not openly. She drank cases and cases of soda, and now weighed over 200 pounds. She was the daughter of Miguel Cecilio, who died not recklessly hunting a dangerous creature with horns, but from a reckless, indiscriminate disease. At least that's what the story says.

1979

Mama must have placed his photo so prominently on the

end table near the entrance to the kitchen, between two fancy candelabras, for a reason. This way, she could look at it inconspicuously and admire it as she wandered through the house each day. This habit of photo worship most likely began when Mama was very young.

1950 (A Story Based on Mama's Stories)

Grandmama Lourdes built a shrine. She kept the shrine for years after Grandpapa's death, dusting and polishing the crosses and frames each week, one at a time. At the time there were plenty of other photos of him. None of them was in color. Some were sepia, others black and white. Mama happened to grab the photo that would become the only surviving one, rescuing it from the fire that burned the entire shrine and all the other photos when she was nine (or ten). The fire was put out in time to save the home and their lives. All of this occurred a short time before Grandmama sent Mama and Auntie Pat away to a Catholic orphanage.

There the nuns were not kind. That's what Mama told me. She said one of the nuns had a crush on a well-developed teenage girl, and that the nun had even touched her. The nun in charge of Mama and Auntie Pat stole some of the valuables that Grandmama had sent along with them in a box—gold and silver necklaces, money, and beautiful stationary for writing letters home. That is why Grandmama never received any letters from her daughters while they grew into young ladies. The nun left the photo of the young girls' father, Miguel Cecilio, alone because it did not appear valuable—neither the photo nor the plastic frame in which it was held.

Josephine slept with the photo under her pillow. She often snuck it out at night after the nuns made their rounds and under the sheet with a small flashlight, she admired the smooth skin and beckoning eyes. She tried to match any memories of her father with the man in the photo, but her attempts failed. She tried to picture the shrine photos before they burned, but the flames always got in the way. In time, the only memory she had was the figure in this one photo.

Mama and Auntie Pat's beds sat side by side, and often, after the nuns made their ritual rounds, the sisters would scoot their beds together into one. Auntie Pat asked for her turn to sleep with the photo under her pillow, not because it was of any real importance to her. As the younger of the two, she wanted only to emulate the older. In fact, being the younger, she felt no kinship with the handsome man in the photo who happened to be her father. But in order to be the good big sister that she knew she should be, Mama acquiesced and hesitantly handed the valued photo to her sister every other night.

1955

At last, in the bloom of their youth, Grandmama removed Mama and Auntie Pat from the orphanage and brought them back home. Josephine, now a teen, lacked the same fervor she had had for the photo of her father and gave it back to her mother, who set it inside a drawer (she couldn't keep it on display as she was now married to another man). The photo survived the passing years of forgetfulness, and somehow ended up once again in Mama's possession.

1980

One day, on her way out the door, Mama forgot to look at the photo. At midday, she tried to see her father as a living, moving being in color, holding her three-year-old self on his knee. She failed. Rather, she saw a large rifle mounted on the wall. When she blinked, the rifle was gone. In its place was an overcoat, which when she approached it in her daydream smelled like medicine and Lysol.

Beyond

There are one or two photos of Mama lying dead in her casket. To this day, I refuse to look at those photos. She's wearing a colorful dress. I only know because I chose the dress in which she was laid to rest. I look at this one surviving photo of Grandpapa Miguel Cecilio. Bushy eyebrows. Full lips. Wavy hair cropped close to the head. Mama's brown eyes.

I see absence. I tell a story. I look again.

ON DEATH, DREAMS, AND MEMORY

"Death is our friend... Life always says 'Yes' and 'No' simultaneously. Death (I implore you to believe) is the true Yea-sayer. It stands before eternity and says only: 'Yes'."

This defense of Death by Rilke still holds a strange power over me, with its aphoristic quality. Despite bordering on the cliché, perhaps these words resonate because of the inevitability of their meaning. Life will give you mixed signals, frustrate you with its ambivalence – "Yes, you can count on me for anything," but "just now I am in over my head." Yet, like a loyal friend, Death offers an eternal bond, says yes and follows through. In the face of forever, Death reaches out to hold you by the hand. I would like to believe Rilke's conviction and follow its lead without fear. I try to resign myself to the eventuality of death, but time and time again, I am haunted by its lengthy list of strategies.

My mother was diagnosed with uterine cancer in 1996. Her doctor described the type as "very rare" (only 5% of women diagnosed with uterine cancer get this aggressive kind). She died within two years of diagnosis. I was nearly 30 at the time, deep into adulthood, but felt like a child who loses her mother too early. She had often asked while she still had strength, "Why me? I've never smoked or drank." She wanted to see the turn of the century but would miss that and so many other things.

Into my mid-thirties I was told that my sisters and I had a 50/50 chance of getting uterine cancer because it is often hereditary. My doctor offered this option in the face of such a high risk: a hysterectomy. Her advice sounded practical and sound: If I submitted to this surgery, then I would decrease my chances of getting uterine cancer down to zero. I didn't want children anyway. But a hysterectomy seemed a drastic step for someone in her thirties with healthy reproductive organs. So, I set the idea aside for the time being.

Find me at age 45 with my current gynecologist proposing the same thing: a total hysterectomy, leaving me with just my ovaries. She bases her recommendation on a pre-cancer screening that identifies my chances of acquiring cancers of all types. I'm given a computer-generated calculation of my risks in the form of percentages, mutation probabilities. Colorectal cancer leads at a lifetime chance of 4%, followed by endometrial (otherwise known as uterine), which, at a lifetime chance of 3%, ranks second. Ovarian cancer shows up, but only at a miniscule .8%. Worry about that later.

With absolute conviction that I still didn't want children, I submitted to the hysterectomy. I felt justified when my doctor found extensive endometriosis in my uterus and the surrounding area. Some doctors claim that endometriosis may lead to cancer of the uterus, or at least heighten the risk. Uterine cancer scratched off the list. Still, taking this action did not absolutely absolve my fears.

My family's history with cancer is extensive. Several years ago, my oldest brother got testicular cancer in his early thirties and was left with one testicle after surgery. Two of my cousins currently have breast cancer, one of them having survived uterine cancer a few years before her breast cancer diagnosis. The most recent case does the most to dishearten, sadden, and daunt me.

My sister's stage IV took her in just three months. She

never smoked a cigarette in her life. Yet I did on and off for years. In fact, when she heard I had picked up the habit during my study abroad in Wales, she called our father and asked why I was smoking and pressured him to say something to get me to stop. What shocked me was not so much that my sister died of cancer, but the type of cancer she got and the age at which she died. She was 48, ten years younger than my mother was when she died.

It didn't take long for me to remember, even though it was a decade ago. I remembered the spot on my lung the doctors had found accidentally. I had gone into the emergency room for severe cramping on my right side. When the ER doctor couldn't find what was causing such intense pain, he ran a CT scan, which revealed a cyst had burst in my ovary. The scan also picked up a spot on my lung. When I was sent to a lung specialist, he measured the spot as very tiny, but advised me to come back in five months to measure any growth. I never did go back. In the interim, I had lost my insurance and simply forgot.

When my sister died, I couldn't shake the feeling that I was the one who deserved it. Not her. She never smoked and out of concern didn't want me to either. I deserved it for my negligence. But I didn't wish to die, whether by these means or any other. So, I complied with my new doctor's orders to have X-rays done when I told her of my past. She said I ought to get my lungs checked, with the strong history of cancer, and with my sister's death. The technician found nothing.

Death by other means. Colon cancer. For several months prior to my surgery, I suffered from increasing stomach troubles, sometimes up to six bowel movements in one day, so that I considered submitting to a colonoscopy. I decided to hold off, maybe because the cost would be hefty, maybe because I feared what they would tell me. Then, after the surgery, I started having headaches at the back of my head, on the left. I researched online. Headaches confined to one location could mean a brain tumor. Or a sign of hormone changes, fibromyalgia, or chewing too much gum. My sister had been suffering headaches, I learned from other family members, for something like five months before her terminal diagnosis. The frequency and intensity of her headaches worsened until they happened daily.

Soon after my hysterectomy, when I had fully awoken, the nurse took me for a walk. With the monitor still attached to my IV, I couldn't help but think of my sister doing the same exact thing, shuffling down the slick shiny floor of the ICU with only part of her mind functioning. My father and I took the short walk with her. The doctors said she had over 30 cancerous lesions in her brain. My mind functioned just fine as I walked the hospital hallway. My mind, in fact, over-functions.

Here I am trying to trace my relationship with Death, the inevitable "friend." In order to do so, I need to reach into the past. I'd much rather let the past go. But to change the dynamic I have with Death, I must understand our personal history.

*

Like everyone else, memories visit my mind either unannounced or by beckoning. I describe them the only way I know how—through narrative. I try to create order out of the menagerie, tame chaos into a coherent story.

I'm five or six years old. I pause on my way to play our

electric organ in the patio and see a powdery substance on the floor. I stoop forward, swipe some onto my fingers, and lick. The pale-yellow powder tastes bitter, the way I imagine my mother's musky perfume might taste. I cough, clutch my throat and wander back into the kitchen. I find myself in the living room instead, Mama and Papa lounging in their respective reclining chairs.

I tell them what happened, that I swallowed something I found on the floor. Maybe straw candy sold at 7-Eleven, the ones with different flavored powders you could shake onto your palm and lick up or directly into your mouth. But no, what I tasted was bitter, not at all sweet or tangy. *Am I'm going to die?*

Death had been this elusive ghostly thing in fairy tales and fables or cartoons on TV. Catch a glimpse—*Sleeping Beauty looks dead, but she isn't really, she's only sleeping* —and with one kiss, love rather than death, becomes the wish. I imagine the logic behind the masking of death, the veneer: *Childhood is fleeting, so let the children savor those few years of security and tranquility.* When I thought I might die from poisoning, Death became nearly real. I realized that I could die, and if I could die so young, so could Mama and Papa. They were, after all, so old. I don't remember them giving me a lecture on death or answering my question, "Will I die?" at all. Instead, all I remember is that Mama gave me my favorite dessert, a Hostess Ding-Dong. Washed down with a tall glass of water. Death had turned real for this little girl. But having been fed doctrines of life after death in addition to cartoon heaven, I was still not fully cognizant of what death would really mean. For the time being, I put those fears behind me.

For a while, Death existed the way the sun and moon

do, or the ocean tides: each did its thing with or without my acknowledgment. It existed the way going to sleep at night and waking up at daylight was a habit that never demanded much thought or contemplation. I could see my future stretch forward like a never-ending road, with so many possibilities along the way. That quiet exuberance always present in my youth, bubbling over. Though I cannot remember with close detail all that I would like of those early childhood years, I relish the overall sense of excitement and wonder, how it kept me afloat even during the most difficult times.

My parents didn't spank me when I was little, but they did spank my older siblings. My mother was the main disciplinarian. Her awful temper often led to her grabbing anything within reach—a vacuum piece or shoe, or belt— and whack it on the exposed leg or arm of my sisters. Then when alone in bed, I'd replay the scene in my head and imagine what it would be like to be spanked, crying so hard that I'd tremble and choke on my own tears. Then I'd stare blindly at the ceiling and imagine my own funeral, predicting who would attend, what they would be thinking, what they would say about me. All those who took me for granted would feel really sorry and it would be too late. I imagined the way in which my family and friends would react to seeing my body in the coffin, down to the detail of how I would be dressed. But if death was really the end, how would I be able to see all of this? Maybe I would still be around in some form or another to observe discreetly? Death just didn't seem like the real end.

From the time my mother had been baptized as a Jehovah's Witness, I had been taught that when you die you are truly dead, no longer able to think, to move, to live in this world. But Death was not something to fear, for you had the promise of the resurrection, where you and all the faithful would arise again, in the same human form. Some would arise as spirits, but my destiny, I was told, was of the earthly kind.

As I grew older, death became more manifest. I'd catch glimpses on the television news that my parents would watch before dinner. They couldn't forever hide from me the reality of people dying, church members and members of their extended family.

One time, in my teen years, when I hadn't yet lost anyone close to me, the old fear returned to me—what if Mama or Papa were to die sometime soon, through some illness or accident? The proposition aroused a melancholic curiosity. What if Mama gets cancer, I wondered, like the series of people in our religion, mostly women, who had died of cancer? Blossom, the wife of one of the elders in our congregation; the Filipina mother of two young belligerent sons; another Filipina woman, whose daughter had run away when the mother got sick, then committed suicide not long after. Yes, by now I had been exposed to the fruits of death, though just by word of mouth. The word cancer took on the sound of a plague that one could catch.

In a kind of delirium, I imagined my mother's funeral, not the color of the coffin or the dress she'd be wearing, but all the people who would be there, what they would say about her, what they would say to me. They'd feel sorry for me, losing my mother while so young. I'd be deeply grieving, yes. But what would it be like without Mama around to restrict me in her overbearing way? My conscience immediately kicked in when my imaginings took this turn, freeform daydreaming reaching its limit, and I felt like a bad person for even considering the possibility. Yes, I wanted the burden of her possessiveness to end, but like this? I could not know at the time that this thought would be a kind of premonition, for a few years later she would be diagnosed with uterine cancer and die from it so quickly.

When the doctor said straight to her face while she sat limp in the wheelchair, "You will die from this," her mouth hung open and her eyes filled with tears. I wish I could say what I felt the moment I witnessed this scene, but I can't. Enraged at the doctor for his thoughtlessness? Complete lack of tact? Frustration? Numbness? When I later pondered the reality of the situation and how the doctor wouldn't say this unless he really knew she couldn't survive, I felt trapped between a nightmare and a daydream, part of me resisting the death sentence, another immersed in the future of tomorrow—life without my mother. And when she told me the day before she died, "Now you can party all you want," her words cut so deeply that I wished to be the one to die, for hadn't I quietly imagined this scenario, hadn't I practically wished something would happen to remove her restraints?

*

The little girl, dressed for school, reaches down and touches the dark brown goo on the carpet. When she sniffs her fingers, the odor makes her wince. Her eyes water. She stands dumbstruck, as if in an impossible dream. Un-thinkingly, she rubs her fingers together so that her hand is mired in the waste now. She walks toward the kitchen, its fluorescent light like a beacon in comparison to murkiness of the room she's now in, which her family calls "Sala" in their native tongue, the living room. The walls are covered in dark brown panel, fashionable in the seventies. The china cabinet, imported from Japan, is also of a dark brown hue, as is the sundial clock hanging above it. The fireplace is decorated with gray stones, and the windows are heavily draped with maroon curtains that are kept closed all night and rarely opened even during the day. The two crystal-ball-shaped lamps hanging from the ceiling give off a dim orange light. Perhaps this atmosphere contributed to the little girl's blindness to what the brown goo really was - the "uht uht" (words again from her family's native tongue), or poop of their hot dog shaped dog, what is his name? She hates this dog because of its nasty habit of licking her back in the summertime when she takes long afternoon naps.

Did the room really give off a hazy darkness, the dark-colored furniture combining to create this overbearing weight upon the little girl about to head to school? Or is this a fictional re-creation of a memory so old that filling in the blanks becomes necessary? The girl cries, and her mother promptly washes her sullied hand and she walks to her school barely in time for the morning bell.

The same little girl hangs onto the neck of her father she calls Papa, wearing a black and white cow print coat. Her eyes are shut as together they whirl on Disneyland's pirate ride. She closes her ears to the echoes of a ghostly voice telling the story of the adventurous pirates, as they pass each installment. The boat goes slowly, but with her eyes closed, it feels like she is whirling. She whispers in Papa's ear, "You're the only man I've ever loved." *But wait? She said this at some point in her life, but did she really say it at this point in time?* She feels her heartbeat esca- lating, and her Papa squeezes her tighter saying, "It's okay, baby." He calls her baby, even till today.

These memories are mine, and I remember them when searching for my feelings about death. Though she's been dead now for almost 17 years, I miss my mother. I contemplate how close death is for my father, who is now 80 years old. Maybe I remember these moments because they captured my senses in powerful ways. And yet, I feel somewhat removed from the little girl who is the focus of these childhood memories. These memories are supposed to help explain me, my life, who I am and who I have become. Yet when I try to inhabit the form in the memory, I don't completely succeed. The sense of my own grown self is here with me, and I cannot shrink in size enough to embody the little girl of my memories. And so, I write as if watching a child enact my past, and I follow her though the fog as closely as I can.

Perhaps I remember these instances in my childhood because they have to do with my fixations with touch, with taste. As an adult, I no longer have an infantile oral fixation, so how can I truly relate? I haven't asked my sister or my parents what they remember—comparing memory notes. I see the Disneyland memory more vividly because of the photo in one of our family albums. I am indeed wearing a black and white cow print coat and holding on tight to Papa's neck. My eyes are closed, his are not. When I first saw the photo, did I already securely possess the memory, the photo serving to ignite it in my mind? I close my eyes and try to remember what it was like in the dark, dank tunnel, and how it felt to hug my father as we whirled around on the ride. Embarrassed that I told him he was the only man I had ever loved. I fail to feel the moment fully. For me, it's just a story. This is me because I'm told it is so, it looks like me, so I must believe.

*

Once in a while, amid the flux and flow of everyday doings, I pause and a quiet panic sweeps over me. I think: *My sister is dead. So young, she is truly gone. What did you think the moment you found out you were terminally ill? Did you panic, lose your breath? Did you want to shout, cry out and damn this world?* Then the feeling dissipates, just like that, or the thought, and I go on with whatever it is I'm doing.

Death can bring you "into absolute and passionate presence with all that is here," moving you to live more fully, love others and give more freely. This is the gist, I think, of Rilke's words. I don't know if I'll ever be able to befriend Death to this extent. I'd like to start fresh, anew. The past is only useful in the form of memories by bringing us back to origins and the fragments that shape what we are. We mold these pieces into the shape of story. We explain our present by means of the past. And what about the future? Yes, even the future depends on our ability to create the world from scraps.

THE THING ABOUT BRUISES
IS THAT THEY HEAL

Papa: beat big sister's legs with one of the long vacuum tubes and then dragged her by the hair. She cowered. This is what we think we remember. It happened in a matter of minutes—two, maybe three.

Mama and Papa: married on leap year. Papa says they eloped. He says they didn't know that it was leap year. Each time he tells this story, we, his children, don't really believe. This same time every year he remembers. She carried a rag doll and wore a yellow dress when he came to take her away from a home that she wanted so desperately to forget.

Regret:

Not knowing is not the same, as not remembering.

Even if someone had taken photos, no one would have believed that this man could have done such a thing. He appears ordinary and sweet.

Who would attribute such cruelty to this man who walks around the house in bare feet? Whose hands used to caress the dog's belly before stirring the homemade soup for his family?

One imagines a child beater as one with a permanent scowl or steel-toed boots on his feet.

Papa doesn't remember exactly what kind of doll Mama held as they held each other in the spare room in the house of his navy mate, or what material the yellow dress was made of or if it was plain or decorated with checkers or flowers, or clasped closed or zipped. He does remember that both the doll and Mama were soft and sweet.

Regret:

Maybe at the same time that he raised the tube, he remembered the splatter of hot oil on the skin of his arms and forehead, the oil left unattended in the frying pan, or the time when his mother made him kneel on salt on the floor while holding several books in both hands. Whenever he tells this story, he makes sure to admit what a naughty little boy he had been.

When he was a naughty little boy in the Philippines, he sang little tunes for the American soldier who handed him a candy bar. He didn't hide in secret hiding places like other little boys in his village. His cousin, the one with the mean streak, kept him safe from bullies and Japanese soldiers and their cruelty. This mean-streaked cousin, older than him by four years, lived into his forties and, not surprisingly, drank consistently.

Papa says he never wielded the tube as an instrument of punishment that day. He says he can't remember – no he could never—do such a thing.

At the time of the alleged beating, Polaroid cameras were in fashion. But they were used (ordinarily) to record happy things: holiday celebrations, birthdays and costume parties.

Regret:
Even if you showed him photos,
bruises don't come easily.

A monkey that belonged to the American soldier bit him in the leg. He didn't kill it or beat it over the head because he was still a little boy and the monkey wasn't his pet.

He now says that keeping pets is really a form of cruelty. Animals were meant to run wild and free.

Papa used to call big sister, when she was small, Little Princess, instead of by her real name. He's surprised that we remember that.

He used to call the occupying soldiers, "those means Japs," each one of them mean and cruel, through and through.

Papa as a little boy, witnessed a Japanese soldier blow off the top of a woman's head. Blow a man's guts outs so that his little son tried for the longest time to hold them in.

Now that he's an old man, Papa, a navy vet, has forgiven them. He doesn't call them names. He doesn't speak much about World War II, or any other war for that matter, but of more ordinary, mundane things.

Regret:

Most often he hides away in his office that is also his bedroom—the one with the doorknob that doesn't have a lock. He keeps the door shut, even though he lives alone, by inserting a little piece of cardboard between the door and the frame. It's not so easily opened.

DEATH—A PLAY

ACT I SCENE 1: THE THEME

(ACTOR and WRITER sit back to back on a yoga mat. WRITER's shoulders are slumped. She wraps her arms around her knees. ACTOR sits in the lotus position with a perfectly straight posture.)

ACTOR: Why am I here?

WRITER: I called you. Don't you remember?

ACTOR: Yes, but why am I really here? I must say, I was quite surprised by your request for an audition. Your script is not yet complete.

WRITER: True, but there's enough here for a beginning.

ACTOR: Or an end. A theme—DEATH.

WRITER: More than just a general abstraction as that. Remember? We spoke about the situation. How Papa is still alive, yet I am already grieving. I am afraid my premature grief is affecting my work. Thus, the unfinished script.

ACTOR: Yes. Yes. Your work is suffering. Because of DEATH. Thus, the theme.

WRITER: I suppose there's no one else to blame but myself for the confusion. After all, I feel compelled to create drama where there may not be any...

ACTOR: *(continued)* Papa is terminally ill, yes? Sure to die sooner than later?

WRITER: Yes. He has been diagnosed with prostate cancer, which has spread to his vital organs. He can no longer taste his food and can no longer walk. He gets around the house in a wheelchair. He refuses any kind of medical treatment (you know him—his resistance to hospitals and doctors), and besides, his doctor suggests that he is too old and frail for treatment anyway. I was about to say...what did I mean to say? I am at an impasse...

ACTOR: *(continued)* Papa is in what you might call...the sunset of his life.

WRITER: Your words, not mine.

ACTOR: Splitting hairs. Mine yours, what is the difference? The point is, at 84, Papa has lived a long, full life. DEATH in this situation is not exactly a surprise.

WRITER: No, it isn't, which makes my early grief all the more unreasonable. That's my head talking, not my heart. I try to call every day. He is over a thousand miles away.

ACTOR: An opportunity for dramatic irony.

WRITER: What's that now? How so?

ACTOR: Dramatic Irony: When there is a gap between what an audience knows and what a character believes or expects. Make it so that your audience does not yet know that Papa is not yet dead, and the first thing they see is— "Act I Scene 1":

(Broken, grieving, ACTOR sits at invisible typewriter, face in hands, sobbing in front of a photo of Papa.)

WRITER: That's good, that's good!

ACTOR: *(ACTOR uncovers face. Eyes are dry.)* I do apologize for my lack of tears. I am a method actor and I must say, I do not feel the depth of sadness that you describe. Papa seems resigned to the inevitable. DEATH is DEATH, whether by accident, or illness, or any other cause. Everyone dies. Whether this person or that, DEATH—as they say—does not play favorite. DEATH is not partial. If love is blind, so is death. At the risk of sounding insensitive, we can say that Papa is merely representative of millions who will—who must—suffer the same fate.

WRITER: Please do try and remember your place. I am the playwright, you are the actor. Your role is to inhabit my words and bring them to life.

ACTOR: Ah, of course; however, will you not allow your lead actor some creative license? After all, without the actor...

WRITER: *(continued)* ...there is no play.

ACTOR: On that cheerful note, let us return to the apparent plot of this script. Papa is dying, we know this, and we wonder why it is so difficult for you, to accept when it is expected and inevitable. Do I have it right?

WRITER: Yes, that's the gist. Though I haven't quite decided on...on...what is the...

ACTOR: *(continued)* Primary conflict?

WRITER: Now who's splitting hairs?

ACTOR: Main Conflict: Can be external or internal. In your case, it appears to be primarily internal, though you could argue that external factors play some role in the protagonist's struggle, such as cultural and social influence. At any rate, the conflict is part and parcel of the plot, which involves more than just action, but a combination of sequence, pacing, and action that shapes the audience's response and interpretation.

WRITER: You sound quite versed in literary terminology. Impressive. Of course, I haven't worked out all the details of the plot just yet. Heck, I'm not even sure what the theme should...

ACTOR: *(continued)* DEATH?

WRITER: You ought to hear yourself, really. You repeat the word DEATH as if it were your mantra, a sacred liturgy. As one versed in literary terms, you should know that something like DEATH is not a theme. DEATH is a topic and a very broad one at that. Let's narrow things down, shall we? DEATH of Papa, not just any father. Not some shadowy vague thing. Not some archetype or stock character. To hell with universality.

ACTOR: But is not one of your goals to engage your audience by portraying a theme they can relate to?

WRITER: Of course.

ACTOR: An audience can only connect if they can relate. Your narrative borrows from the very tradition you despise, to draw in your audience, a universal theme. Like it or not, DEATH. It comes for us all.

WRITER: DEATH and taxes.

ACTOR: A truism, a platitude. Something so obvious or trite that pointing it out is pointless. Do I have it right?

WRITER: Yes. Too obvious to mention.

ACTOR: I will mention it anyways: Only two things in life are certain—DEATH and taxes. So why resign oneself to one and not the other? Waste energy and emotion on something you cannot change?

WRITER: *(sarcastically)* What would you oh wise one, suggest?

ACTOR: I am glad you ask. Channel your energies to the cares of the living and let the Dead be dead.

WRITER: Which brings us back full circle. Of course, that's what I'd like to do, but it's obviously not so simple. For one thing, I already said that Papa is not yet dead. That is why we are here, you and I, back-to-back, mind to mind. Mind hears the logic, but heart... *(Clasps hands over heart)* After all, I am only human.

ACTOR: *(sings)* "I'm only human, born to make mistakes." One of our favorites.

WRITER: Yes, yes. Another one: *(Together)* "I can't go on I'll go on." What about "Rage against the dying light."

ACTOR: Bah humbug!

WRITER: Resist, resist.

ACTOR: You do go on. I must say, I will never understand the human propensity for redundancy. Why you'd think it was the end of the world rather than the end of just one life. You do not seem to learn from the past. I will never understand.

WRITER: Maybe that's because you are not human, after all.

ACTOR: *(turns around so that they are now face to face)* Look at me: Am I not you?

WRITER: Yes, of course. I really had no other choice.

ACTOR: Foil for your most human sentiments.

WRITER: *(perks up, sits straight and places hands on ACTOR's shoulders)* That's it!

ACTOR: Like the digressions in the heroic poem, Beowulf, in the most unexpected places: The poet tells terrible King Heremod's story as foil, anti-thesis, to highlight the virtues of our brave title hero. *(Closes eyes)* Why am I here?

WRITER: I called you. Don't you remember? I asked you to audition for the part.

ACTOR: The part...of foil?

WRITER: *(speaks in a softened tone)* Come now, you are much more than just that. You fill a supporting role, yes. But you're great at stepping in and out of character, just like that. See things objectively, as you do so splendidly, so difficult for me...I haven't quite decided yet, but enough. Let us return to the original subject with which this all began. I called and requested an audition and you accepted, with some hesitance.

ACTOR: *(absentmindedly)* Yes, yes. And how am I doing so far?

WRITER: Splendidly. You took a limited amount of information and ran with it. Now tell me, what more do you have to offer in the way of originality? I'd like to see your talent. Anything you like.

ACTOR: I would very much like if my performance would perhaps serve as subtheme to the main theme—for cannot a narrative have more than one theme?—which we agreed is DEATH.

WRITER: Well see here, I never agreed...oh never mind. How about I give you a role and scene and you give me what you can. How about I play my dying father and you be me.

ACTOR: Splendid. I can do that.

WRITER: *(clears throat)* Baby, have you read my love letters to your mother yet?

ACTOR: Letters? No Papa, I haven't. Do you want me to?

WRITER: Oh yes, that's why I gave them to you after all. *(Steps out of character)* Good, good. You have it right. I-- we call him Papa, don't we?

ACTOR: Yes, of course, of course, though it always made us feel a little but uncomfortable, especially when he used that term of endearment in public. And they both--Papa and Mama--demanded that we address them as Papa and Mama, rather than as Mother, Father, or Mommy and Daddy.

WRITER: You, yes, you're right. You know me better than I imagined. You are probably wondering what Papa's letters to Mama has to do with anything. I'm just going with my gut here. I suppose we will see. The point here is progress, process...

ACTOR: *(continued)* Perfect. I asked for a subtheme, which I have faith will be illuminated by this most curious subplot.

WRITER: I'm not totally convinced that the obstacle to our moving on has to do with Papa dying as it has to do with something else entirely. Death at an old age should make things easier. It should be easier to accept than say, a loved one's untimely death, like sister's. She died at 48, and it did not take...very long for me to get over.

(There's an uncomfortable silence for a long few seconds.)

ACTOR: Now, now, one guilt-trip at a time. No one gets to choose how they will die, unless of course they commit suicide. Millions of people die from cancer every year, one of the leading causes of human death, no? Death by cancer, even if at a younger age is not entirely unexpected.

WRITER: Come now, stop intellectualizing everything. Logic and reasoning have their place, but I'm not so sure they do when it comes to matters of the heart. Why does my heart ache so just thinking of Papa passing, yet this same heart hardly ached when sister died?

ACTOR: If what you experienced (or failed to) with sister was not a matter of the heart, then perhaps it was a matter of religion.

WRITER: Meaning?

ACTOR: Come on, let us not play innocent. You know exactly what that means. Christians say that to grieve is to be weak. Christians expect to see their loved ones again in some form, whether in heaven or earth, in some paradisiac realm. If they believe this with all their mind and heart, then their grief is only passing, and they praise God—for heaven hath one more flower. At the fated hour, they will be reunited with their loved one once again. All this to say that perhaps you did not mourn sister because you believe. You have faith.

WRITER: You know us better than that. We may have been full of faith once, but we lost our religion long ago. *(Together)* "Losing my religion!"

ACTOR: I always sensed some proclivity for spirituality. Now that we are face to face, it makes perfect sense.

WRITER: How so?

ACTOR: Call it a sixth sense, though I am not much for the obscure.

WRITER: What? You've demonstrated quite literally an affinity for generalization. But let us lay our differences to rest. Back to the subject at hand: I do not believe in any kind of hereafter.

ACTOR: Neither do I.

WRITER: Of course not. I haven't quite worked out your character arc. I'm not sure there's room for such contextual exposition, such world-building in a stage play like this.

ACTOR: Let us return to the primary issue. You are trying to figure out why you cannot let go of dear old Dad—forgive me, dearest Papa. If it is not because you lack faith, or because you are weak, then...this is my character arc, my purpose. I am trying to fulfill my role, the gist of which is to play my part in getting us closure. Since we do not believe in a hereafter, we cannot accept that we will never see dear old Dad again.

WRITER: Papa, it's Papa. But perhaps yes, if it isn't because of Christian weakness or failure to combine faith with feeling.

ACTOR: Perhaps it is after all, LOSS. I get that, to an extent. We will miss Papa.

WRITER: Maybe.

ACTOR: The letters. Act II.

WRITER: I will decide what comes next. I am in charge.

ACT I: SCENE 2: THE LETTERS

WRITER: I think it time for a soliloquy. Step into character please.

ACTOR: Certainly. *(Clears throat)* I will try.

WRITER: Good, you have it. Always clearing my throat. Sounds much like "smoker's cough." Sister died of lung cancer, when I was certain I was the one who must have had it. I smoked on and off. She never touched a single cigarette.

ACTOR: Very well then: "Today is the anniversary of my sister's death. Four years to be exact. I remember getting the text. It was the day before Valentine's, and I was sitting at the breakfast table. After silently reading the text, I turned to my husband, who asked what the matter was. I did not cry, so perhaps he could tell by the look in my eyes. I read to him the message word for word. He came from behind and rubbed my shoulders, even though I was not crying. I never did."

WRITER: That was good and true to life. I think however that we should go even further back; my lack of what you might call a normal response to sister's death began elsewhere and earlier. Here, let me show you: "My husband was driving on our road trip to Kansas for Thanksgiving. I got the phone call with the results of my sister's tests. She had cancer, lung, and the lesions had spread to her brain. What happened next felt scripted, as if I was being directed by ulterior expectations for terrible news like this. I threw the phone and screamed. "My sister, she has cancer." And we didn't speak for the rest of the trip.

ACTOR: You are being too hard on us. We were not all that close.

WRITER: I'm not finished. When she died three months later, I posted this to my social media wall: "In memory of my sister who died, just short of her wedding anniversary." That was it and I added a photo I borrowed from a relative because I did not own a photo of my deceased sister. Condolences from close and distant friends, from friends of friends, essentially strangers. I had also posted a tribute—remember?—to Cleo. She had to be put down due to cancer a couple of months prior: "In memory of my precious fur baby, who stood by me for 8 years, through single-life trials, through getting my graduate degree. Sweet precious kitty." See, Facebook reminds me on the anniversary of both their deaths, my sister and my cat. The memorial tribute word count for pet longer than for sister.

ACTOR: We were not close.

WRITER: No, I suppose we weren't.

ACTOR: You cannot choose your family, nor can you choose who you love.

WRITER: Another aphorism, another platitude. It's been less than a year and I do not mourn anymore for sister. Papa is not even dead yet, and I already mourn.

ACTOR: Are you sure this is grief you are experiencing, or is it altogether something else, something gnawing at you just under the surface, enough to make you feel guilty for feeling something inappropriate? You are about to lose someone you actually love. But before he goes, is there something you want to say?

WRITER: To him, or to myself, or to someone else? To no one at all? I don't know. I don't know. Something tells me...

ACTOR: The Letters.

WRITER: Fine then. Let us begin. "Joji Dearest, I couldn't find the right phrases to define the feelings in me. As if I'm lost in a place of nowhere. I don't know what to think or what to believe. For the first time in my life I felt like a child lost and deprived."

ACTOR: Excuse the interruption, but are you still playing Papa and I, you?

WRITER: *(annoyed)* Yes, that is the idea.

ACTOR: Would you like me to play you reading Papa's letter?

WRITER: Fine. I suppose that would make more sense.

ACTOR: If I could make a suggestion.

WRITER: What is it?

ACTOR: Have you thought of using letters that reveal something interesting about Papa?

WRITER: Fine then. How about this one, written 5 Jan. 1960 2:10 P.M. If the navy taught Papa anything, it was to be precise. The backstory as told to us by Papa (several times): The main obstacle to Mama and Papa's marriage was apparently Grandma Lourdes. She did not want Joji to marry Manny, and Manny was deeply in love (infatuated?) with Joji—Josephine. They eloped after knowing each other for only three months. They didn't know it was leap year. That Mama took her doll with her and wore a yellow dress. How they stayed at Uncle's house that night. How it was all so sweet.

ACTOR: "Joji, darling, I love you so much, and for even a moment I couldn't see you seems to be a decade. If your mom could only understand, perhaps she'll give me a chance right then. I'm not saying anything against her for mothers are always like that...to seek what is good for their children. But as I had told you beforehand, the situation I'm in, somebody got to give."

WRITER: I think he meant to say, "something's got to give." But of course, English is Papa's second language. He always asks us to edit his letters before he sends them off.

ACTOR: And?

WRITER: For the longest time, I resisted reading the letters. After Mama died of cancer, Papa gave me the letters and I stowed them away in my treasure trunk telling myself that someday in the distant future I would finally read them. Mama's death was still fresh and so I couldn't face anything to do with the memory of her, not yet, not the photos of her in the casket that sister kept at her house and asked if I wanted to see, and certainly not the love letters. I was afraid the letters would reveal an irretrievable past. Now that I have read them, they verify what I suspected: How Papa knew Mama was the one right away, and how they were—at least to him—so in love. Something Mama told me years ago still haunts me. She said, "When we got married, I wasn't really in love. I grew to love Papa over time." This helps explain why there are no available letters from her to him. The longing, the anxiety, the frustration in between the lines, all coming from him.

ACTOR: Which is to say, you never truly know anybody.

WRITER: Which is to say, I ask myself, in some ways, was their marriage a lie?

ACTOR: Is there something else about our Papa you regret?

WRITER: Maybe. Perhaps the real theme of this play is "DEATH—A Life."

ACTOR: Please no, that sounds too pretentious.

WRITER: If you think that, then why go on? You responded to my request for an audition because something about this specific script called to you, the essentials of our story, the drama, the play.

ACTOR: True. Because this play explores one of the most universal themes, the same story, just our version.

WRITER: Well why answer the call to this version?

ACTOR: Because it is a play. And I am an actor on a stage, even if it may be ramshackle, artificial. Now that we have come this far, we have got something to work with and you are approaching some kind of story, a familiar theme...

WRITER: Don't say it.

ACTOR: *(silent)* ...

WRITER: DEATH, and why it matters.

ACT I: SCENE 3: CLOSURE

(ACTOR and WRITER are sitting face to face. Their fore-heads touch and their hands are on each other's shoulders.)

WRITER: Before you go, Papa, I want to say something.

ACTOR: What is it baby?

WRITER: I'm gonna just come out and say it. When big sis was a teenager, you got so mad at her. I don't even remember what she did, but you took a vacuum tube and beat her legs with it.

ACTOR: What? No, that isn't true. That never happened.

WRITER: Well that's what I remember. Strike that. That never happened. The memory, yes. But not the confrontation. I could never confront him like that. I don't like discomfort that comes with confrontation; therefore, this couldn't have happened.

ACTOR: So, we are going with memoir, autobiography.

WRITER: Whatever. Maybe. I don't like labels.

ACTOR: This is it. This is what's bothering you, among other things. You need to confront him before he passes. Please.

WRITER: Maybe you're more courageous than I. Besides, what good would it do to bring up something like that, that happened so long ago. Let the past be the past.

ACTOR: Well then, I think I am ready.

WRITER: For what?

ACTOR: For my real audition. For the finale.

WRITER: Good. Good. Let's have it.

ACTOR: "Oh, look at the moon, all shining up there. Oh, how she looks like a lamp in the air."

WRITER: Oh, I remember that little ditty. The first time Papa sang it, he did so from memory. He said he remembered it from his grandmother in the Philippines. One of the many stories he told us. We were but a small child the first time we heard it, wearing a cow-print coat and hanging onto his neck. There's a photo of that, which proves that it really happened. We whispered something like, "You're the only man I've ever loved," into his ear.

ACTOR: *(so touched and moved, begins to weep)* We so looked up to him, didn't we? Before time and life revealed to us that our parents, like us, are only human. Sorry, that is so out of character.

WRITER: *(touched and moved, begins to weep too)* That's fine, really. You know, you and I, we are the same. We are only human, after all.

THE WAKE OF OUR FORGETTING

The service is to begin at 10:00 a.m., one of several scheduled for this busy December weekend. We are the first to arrive: Little Brother, my husband, and me. Papa's coffin is draped with an American flag and sits atop a sturdy lowering device. Three groundskeepers with their sun hats and gloved hands loiter nearby. Are they ready? Are we?

As I tread over the green turf, I am startled by Mama's marker propped up a few feet behind Papa's coffin. *Here lies Josephine C. Cabrera. In our hearts forever. The resurrection we await.* And I remember. I remember what the Family Service Counselor had said just last week: "Don't worry, your mother will not be disturbed by the disinterment. Her casket is sealed in a slab of concrete."

Only twelve chairs are set out, for we do not expect a large crowd. Everything is some shade of green: the chairs, the artificial turf, the tarp, Mama's marker (I had picked it, right? The color, the substance, the words. Yes, Papa had asked me to. But this isn't about Mama now is it?).

The next to arrive is Big Brother. He can only stay for the service and not the tribute-to-Papa lunch, for he and his wife must catch their flight home immediately after. Big Sis, the oldest, arrives shortly after with her husband, daughter, and son-in-law in tow.

An older gentleman walks up to us wearing dark sunglasses that sit snug atop a bushy moustache and a black fedora that matches his black suit with red silk tie. He greets us with a handshake and says he's the director, pointing to his lapel. His name is, what's his name? "I'm here in place of Elizabeth." That's right. "I just lost my father this past weekend," she had said, while escorting us on a tour of the cemetery grounds. "Oh no," we responded in sympathetic unison. I couldn't believe the coincidence. Her empathy did not go unnoticed. I said, "If you don't mind me asking, what did your father die of?" Taken aback perhaps by the directness of my question, she did not immediately reply. She said, "My father had been in declining health for years, you know, a shutdown—one by one—of the main physical processes." Papa also suffered a lengthy decline, though his was from a slow-growing prostate cancer that went undetected for years because he had stubbornly refused to see a doctor.

When Big Brother places a wreath of carnations on top of the coffin, the director tells him to remove it, "Nothing is to be placed on top of the flag." The flag a shroud obscuring from view the make and model of the casket we had chosen based on Papa's wishes: Batesville Delray, light pecan satin exterior, rose-tan crepe interior, species of wood unnamed. Papa had made three stipulations for his burial: One, that he be buried on top of Mama and if that wasn't possible, to be buried nearby; two, that he be buried in the simplest, most modest of containers: a wooden box; and three that he not be embalmed. He faithfully followed the Jewish faith—Colel Chabad to be specific—but had never fully converted; one must be denied three times, a challenge for most let alone someone in such poor health. All moot for the Honor Guard detail assigned to this Saturday morning service; all they know about this deceased retired military man is what they need to know to carry out their duty of paying military tribute: Manuel V. Cabrera served in the navy for 22 years, retired as a Chief Machinist, and with a rank of E-7 deserves the 21-gun salute.

But first...

Eulogy

Big Brother had meant no disrespect when he placed the wreath of flowers on top of the American flag and so immediately apologized. He might be ignorant of military protocol, but not of what matters most to our father. Papa retired from the navy over 40 years ago, and though some of the stories he told involved his military experience, most of them emphasized other aspects of his life, such as how he met our mother and his poverty-stricken childhood during World War II in the Philippines.

After removing the flowers, Big Brother returns to the seating area and stands at ready. Any time now he will start the service off with a eulogy. When I asked him to deliver the eulogy, he was just as willing as he had been for Mama's memorial. He said, "I hope it's okay with you guys, but I don't want to focus so much on Papa himself as on what he did for us his children. I'd like to emphasize our gratitude for our friends displaying such kindness in showing up to support us." In a bow tie and golden-colored suit and with a gentle smile, Big Brother begins by introducing "Manuel Valencia Cabrera...better known as Papa...born on November 16, 1934...lived to be the ripe old age of 84 years and some dozen days." He describes Papa in terms of his relationship to others: as father, as husband of "our Mama," and as grandfather to eight grandchildren; as expected, he states who Manuel is survived by. Most effortlessly, he transitions into scripture: "Ecclesiastes 7 verse 1 says: 'A good name, or reputation, is better than good oil, and the day of death is better than the day of birth.' Why? Because on the day of a person's death, that person has accomplished much."

"What do you want me to say about Papa?" he had asked me and Little Brother as his hands hovered over the laptop keyboard in Papa's living room. "He was generous," I said. Little Brother, the youngest of us five surviving siblings, simply nodded in agreement. "And selfless," I added. Papa had, especially in his later years, always vocalized his concern for the well-being and health of his children, dismissing his own discomfort by repeatedly saying, "I'm okay," even when he was not. He had had to catheter himself the past two years at least twice a day and his leg had swollen to twice its size.

"He was a good father and a good husband. And he did all he could in his later years to make sure that he was not a burden to his children." So concerned was he with the welfare of his children that in his living trust he left no stone untouched. With reference to his Mazda RX-8 (evidence of a *late-life* crisis I had teased):

"At the time after my death, ownership of this car shall be transferred under a very simple suggested rule:

1) Flip-coin

2) Draw-straw

3) Whatever all of you decide. Whichever, you can come-up with that's fair......whoever is the winner get the ownership of the car. I love you all, Manuel V. Cabrera/Father."

He had addressed this memo to "All My Children," an addendum which was to override the original memo dated four years earlier; that document had originally transferred ownership only to his two youngest children—me and Little Brother, who were to:

"1) Sell the car and split 50/50

2) Either one may offer the other to pay half of the price (Kelly Blue Book at that time)

3) Flip a coin...whoever wins...got to keep the car

At any rate.... may the both of you be content and at peace with one another.... whichever option you wish to take."

Two years after the most recent memo his RX-8 was wrecked in an accident and he bought a more modest car—a Honda hybrid—to take its place. We didn't need to flip a coin or draw straws or any such method for in his final days, Papa decided to give the car to Big Sis, the only one of his children living locally. He transferred ownership to her with the caveat that she let her siblings use it when visiting. We had recently coordinated our visits with the intent of parsing out responsibility for Papa's care since he refused hospice care. None of us were to come at the same time to ensure coverage for stretches of time beginning in winter and ending in late spring. The plan was that Big Brother was to come first, followed by me, Little Brother and then by the second to the oldest, Other Big Sis. Papa took a turn for the worse sooner rather than later, so we each arranged to come as soon as we could. I flew in first on a Tuesday night (just hours before his death) followed by Big Brother, Other Big Sis, and lastly Little Brother, who all happened to arrive after he died. Papa's car was stored in his garage, the keys for which Big Sis kept hanging by the door for whoever was visiting now. We still called it Papa's car even though he hadn't driven in years and it was no longer his.

Big Brother continues: "Papa was reclusive after Mama's death, but he wasn't always." He fondly remembers the family station wagon (*we had a wagon?),* the green and white camper (that I vaguely remember, laying down on the compact bed), and how Papa used to take his children to the beach and camping. I don't remember any of those trips, but I do remember going to the drive-in to see two very scary B-movies, one about a man who turns into a snake (or a snake who turns into a man), and another one called "Bugs," about well, an epidemic of bugs. Were those the days when Mama and Papa were still kind of fun?

"He loved his family. Papa loved his children. Even Jesus, who promised to raise the dead, gave way to tears. So today we give way to tears. But we are also not left brokenhearted or crushed in spirit because Jehovah says in Psalms 147 that he heals the brokenhearted, and he binds up their wounds. Those that are here are here to express words of consolation and sympathy. Your presence is greatly appreciated. Take the time," Big Brother says with powerful feeling, "to consider how brief that life is." *How uncertain it is.* "Psalm 90 verse 10 says that the span of our life is 70 years. Or 80 if one is especially strong. So apparently, Papa was especially strong. But as it states further in that same Psalm, they are filled with trouble and sorrow. Yes, my father was filled with trouble, as we all are, we struggle in this life...But the Bible also holds out hope. First Thessalonians chapter 4 says, We do not want you to be ignorant concerning those who are asleep in death, that you may not sorrow just as the rest do who have no hope." *Job, who suffered long, longed for the grave as reprieve after having lost everything.* "Can a man who dies live again? Job answers that yes, he can, and he will wait for God to call him back up from the grave." *Imagine that—our Creator longs to bring the dead back to life. That is the hope that the Bible holds out. Imagine that, imagine what Revelation 21 says, that death will be no more. Neither will mourning, nor outcry, nor pain be anymore.*

Big Brother concludes with, "an expression I'm going to borrow from a scholar and hope this will help us to find comfort from this day forward and the days ahead: While graveyards like this graveyard may remind us of the brevity of life, the resurrection hope that the Bible holds out ensures us of the brevity of death."

If only. Who is this scholar? I thought he was going to quote from Rush, his favorite band, but with the mention of the resurrection, the words must be from a fellow Jehovah's Witness. What would Papa have thought if he could listen to his own eulogy? I should have given the eulogy, considering I was the closest to Papa, or so it seemed, or at least added a few words of my own. Of how Papa was not a Christian but a Noahide and aspiring Jew. How he thought the JW's beliefs were false and how I wasn't sure if before his death he still believed in a resurrection or that he would ever see our mother again. I'm such a coward, just as I was at Mama's funeral. I had not stepped up even though I had the ability to speak as eloquently as Big Brother with his many years of being a congregation elder. But no—my job was to write the poem for the memorial stationary, and Big Brother did his job, didn't he? As trustee, hadn't I had the courage to ask him to take charge? Soon they will lower my dear Papa into the earth on top of our dear Mama, whose grave had to be disturbed according to Papa's wishes.

When Big Brother spoke of the hope of a resurrection—predicted for generations while never coming to fruition—I cringed; Papa subscribed to Jewish belief and was highly opposed to what he called, "That lie of Christianity!" He devoted himself to the Noahides, a peculiar version of Kabbalah. But quoting from the Psalms, that was okay, wasn't it? Papa may have condemned the New Testament, but he believed strongly in the Old, especially the book of Psalms. On every birthday he promised he would read the number Psalm that matched his age to show devotion to "the only true God, the God of Abraham, Isaac, and Jacob." He read one of these Psalms to me one birthday season and it went one ear out the other. Papa may have failed to convert to Judaism, but in his old age, his mind was still sharp. "I'm gonna relocate to Israel, God willing. If only he give me a few more years of life." He used to say, "I'm going to live to 120," and boy that wouldn't be a surprise. *You just keep going, Papa, you're so strong.*

Little Brother and I regularly visited Papa on summer and winter breaks, so we were familiar with Papa's habits, how he donated to Jewish charities on a monthly basis. Just days after his death, I went through his files for important papers and found a letter addressed to Mr. Cabrera, asking for him to "please be as generous as you possibly can" to Jewish children hospitalized in Israel for life-threatening diseases. In the margins, Papa had penned a little note: "A little amount for hospitalized kids in Israel." The note was dated six days before his death in the amount of $25 and included the account number. Papa was very meticulous about keeping accurate records for everything. Papa must have known that he was dying.

Hadn't Big Sis said so? Papa said two nights before his death, "I don't think I'm going to make it." Papa had mentioned something about a rabbi—hadn't he? Was it that I ought to inform the rabbi of his death? But what for? To simply inform? Or to request that he be at Papa's service? To speak? To give his blessing? Do the Noahides or the Chabad believe in an afterlife? What does it matter now that Papa is gone? But if that's what he had wanted, shouldn't I have made sure to make note of it? Was I a selfish daughter for not keeping as accurate a record of his wishes as possible? *And death will be no more. Neither mourning, nor outcry, nor pain be anymore. In our hearts forever, the resurrection we await.* Those words on Mama's marker created by me when I once believed. Hadn't I wished with all my heart that Mama be spared by Jehovah from dying a painful death? "I won't live to see the year 2000." She didn't. Papa would not live to see his great grandchildren or his youngest son's children. He wouldn't see me turn 50 in just a couple of months.

Big Brother did the best anyone could under the circumstances, not knowing if Papa wanted a religious service, or whether he would be offended by a Christian-flavored sermon. But I knew, didn't I? Shouldn't I have told Big Brother about Papa's poor opinion of what he believed to be Truth? Papa probably had told either me or Little Brother at some point what he wished in that regard. What did he wish? What did he wish?

Military Tribute

Other Big Sis watches the whole thing through an iPad sitting on a chair of its own next to Big Sis, who monitors it throughout. Other Big Sis watches with her husband and two kids, set a box of tissue next to her, just in case. She feels numb as she had when Mama died. At Mama's funeral, she only cried when she saw middle sister—who died from lung cancer four years ago at the age of 48—wail and shake upon the lowering of the coffin into the ground. And now through a computer screen she watches and listens to everything—the eulogy, the military tribute, her sisters trembling as they participate in the flower tribute. When the service is over and the screen goes dark, she will whisper goodbye, the lone bugle still echoing in her ears as she heads to the kitchen to prepare dinner.

Little brother is to accept the flag and the rounds on our behalf. When the funeral arranger asked who would accept the flag, we volunteered him. When we asked if he'd like to take the flag home to Korea, he said with directness—"What am I supposed to do with it?"

An Honor Guard team of three stand at ready with their rifles some 50 yards away. Two active duty Honor Guards—one male and one female— stand by the casket at ready and the director begins speaking:

"This does not come easy for many, very special. I see he put many years into the military. The reason I know that is because I see the ones with the rifles. They'll be doing a volley; it gets noisy. We don't have any kids, so it's okay, they won't get scared. I cover my ears usually. During the playing of the taps, I'm going to ask those that can will stand and offer the proper salute, all current and former military members. All others will place their hands over their hearts."

At this time, it gives me great privilege to give you the United States Navy Honor Guard."

Two guards: Step 1-2-3-4-5-6-7-8-9, about face. Lift, fold. About face, salute. Ready, face.

Honor Guard Captain calls to attention, port arms: Ready, to, aim, fire. Ready, to, aim fire. Ready, to, freeze it.

"Family, please stand."

Bugler plays Taps: Da da da, da da da, da da da, da da da, da da da, da da da, da da da, da da da.

"You may be seated."

Two Guards fold the flag: Reach, smooth, fold, left, step side side, fold, fold, fold, fold, fold, fold fold, fold, fold, fold, fold, fold, fold, smooth, tuck, turn over, tuck, press, flatten, lift. Slow salute. Female guard turns, step, step, step, kneels before Little Brother.

"On behalf of the President of the United States, the United States Navy, and our grateful nation, please accept this flag as a symbol of our appreciation for your loved one's honorable and faithful service."

When the guard hands Little Brother the flag, he nods, takes the flag onto his lap, and whispers thank you.

Salute. March away.

Honor Guard Captain strides toward the casket, pauses for one final silent payment of respect. Turns, walks slow with head bowed, then knees before Little Brother.

"On behalf of the United States Navy, please accept these rounds as a symbol of our Navy's core values: Honor, Courage, Commitment."

Little Brother slips the rounds of *honor, courage, and commitment* into his right pocket. Slow Salute, turn. March away.

*

Little Brother wasn't supposed to come until the first of the new year, but then we informed him of Papa's rapid decline, so he flew in earlier. Not early enough. He missed Papa's death because he was tied up with exams. Couldn't he do as I did and have someone else proctor finals? Yes, but then how would he get the written exams over to the US from Korea afterward for grading? At least he wouldn't miss the funeral, which could not be scheduled until 10 days after Papa's death.

He does not cry at the service; he does not cry when I lean on his shoulder and weep. He's not one for tears. In fact, when he got the news of Papa's death, it was my sister-in-law who he says broke down in tears. He does not cry at lunch after the service at Papa's favorite Greek food restaurant, where he accompanied Papa a dozen or more times until Papa could not summon the strength to leave the house. Maybe he cries when alone in the master bedroom where no one has slept since Mama's death, not even Papa who slept in his office-turned-bedroom. No one has stayed in that room except for Other Big Sis who had to return home the same day Little brother arrived. Like Little Brother, she is not much for public displays of feeling. She had no reservations about staying in the room where our mother suffered, and which Papa left undisturbed like a shrine. Unlike the rest of us, Other Big Sis didn't have a specific duty assigned to her. However, she played a big role in getting Big Sis, Big Brother, and me to agree to a visitation of Papa at the funeral home. As the first one to rouse the courage, she implored, he looks so peaceful, and much better than in recent photos. In those virtual photos he's wearing his baby blue and red sweat suit, the clothes he died in, hooked up to an oxygen machine. Big Sis and I had forewarned her, "Papa will just be covered with a sheet—it might be a difficult thing to see." But she insisted she wanted to see him. Since she had not been there when he died, she wanted to see him one last time. Big Brother had also decided he didn't want to see, for what was the point? And Baby Brother didn't need to decide for he was still out of the country. But at the last minute, Big Brother decided he ought to be there for his family, when he saw how torn up we were over the whole thing. After some twenty minutes, and after wiping tears and blowing noses, we handed over the paper bag of Papa's things we thought should go with him: his nicest pair of black boots, black Bolo Tie, pair of dark gray socks, black faux leather vest, a blue long-sleeved striped shirt, and a pair of black Docker pants. "Papa was so short, look how short the pants are," Other Big Sis had exclaimed. The dead must be dressed in their best. Big Sis gingerly touched Papa's things. She and I carefully recorded the items one by one. I signed the papers as witness to the few items we believed Papa would wish to be buried with. As we left the mortuary, we saw the same ally cat we had seen when we arrived, lounging by the wheel of a white car. All the cars in the parking lot were white. It felt good to breathe in unstifled air. Immediately after, we grabbed lunch from Papa's favorite place for fish tacos; he used to eat at least two. Later of course, he could barely finish one. It made me very sad to see a Styrofoam container with left-over tacos and bottles of Ensure that I thoughtlessly threw out so that Little Brother scolded, "You could have donated them to a food bank!"

Flower Tribute

The flag. The flag is draped over the coffin. Inside lies our dear Papa. The flag drapes the coffin—surprisingly small—so that the only visible part is a sliver of wood. We'd mutually agreed on the most inexpensive wooden coffin, for that is what Papa had wanted—that he should be buried in a wooden box and that the box not cost a lot. Papa affectionately called me Baby from the time I was born to the time of his death. I used to get embarrassed by this nickname, but over time it had become old hat. I sit in the front row between Little Brother and my husband. I hold the phone below eye-level so I can witness the event in real-time while also filming the thing. What for? In case memory—and it will—fails me. The entire military service takes no more than ten minutes, but every few seconds, I look at the screen, and then at the performance in real-time. Sobbing ever so quietly, I lean against Little Brother's stoic shoulder. Now I am embraced by my husband. Inside the wooden coffin Papa lies still. *Will not disturb.* Out of refrigeration for several hours, transported in a black hearse, the opposite of the white van in which Papa was transported freshly dead from his house to the mortuary where he would not be embalmed.

The director announces that next on the agenda is the flower tribute and I immediately raise my hand before he finishes speaking. "It's a tradition, symbolic. It's what we call a flower tribute. It's a way of saying, Manuel, we loved you. Manuel, we're gonna miss you. And I think it's been touched on, till we see each other again. Can I have two family members." I want to lay the wreath of flowers on top of the coffin, the flowers sent from Uncle, Papa's one surviving brother of the Cabrera clan in the Philippines. I wonder how long the flowers will last beneath the soil and grass and how long before Papa's un-embalmed body will begin to decay. I remember because it happened so recently: Uncle Junior's response to seeing his brother hooked up to the oxygen machine, unconscious, all through the smart phone screen. How he insisted, "I want to speak to my brother," even after I tried to tell him that his dear brother was dying. Uncle simply couldn't believe it was true. "I just spoke to him two weeks ago, on his birthday," he insisted, "He said he was fine." But Papa always said he was fine, up until that Sunday before his death I spoke to him one last time, I had a feeling it would be, shaking and crying unconsolably. Hearing my sobs, he had said in a soft, weak voice, "I'll be okay." I insisted, "No you won't. You need help. Please accept the help offered by"—*dare I say the word of death*—"hospice." I tried to calm Uncle down by saying, "You can speak to Papa, if you want, I will bring the phone over to him." I brought my phone to the hospital bed set up in the living room, the TV behind it on to some cable channel with the volume on low (who turned it on, probably the hospice nurse to keep the motif from being too solemn and dark), faced the screen to where Uncle could see Papa and Uncle burst out, "Oh no, my brother, Manoy, no!" Then I brought the phone to Papa's ear. Uncle spoke in their shared dialect of Cebuano, his voice having lowered, words I could not understand, but could imagine. *Manoy, brother, please, this cannot be. I love you Manoy, I love you so much.* It was all too much to bear, I returned to the kitchen as if out of fear that this would be all too much for Papa, who the nurses had reassured us could still hear. The almost-dead, comatose-like patient can still hear; the sense of hearing is the last to go. "We used to play when we were boys," Uncle Junior said, defeated, "Manoy, Boy." He was so distraught that I worried he might have a heart attack, considering the shock and his poor health. So, I messaged my aunt the next day to ask after Uncle and she said that his blood pressure was high all that day but finally lowered. "Your Uncle Junior is better, thank the lord."

I and Big Sis, youngest and oldest girls respectively, step toward the flag-draped coffin and lay the wreath gently atop. As I step down from the threshold, I look down into the pit where Mama is buried, deeper than six feet. As together we lay the wreath of carnations down on the coffin, I tremble with tears and remove my glasses to wipe my eyes. I whisper words of endearment to Papa and sit back down next to Little Brother, the flag folded on his lap with only the white stars on display. While his duty was to accept the flag, mine was to write a poem for the memorial stationary. Aside from Little Brother, I am the only sibling who professes to be a writer and so it was a given that I'd create the poem in Papa's memory. I didn't want to express just my thoughts and feelings (and what were they exactly), so I asked each sibling to contribute one line each, say, their fondest memory. In the end, I relied on the stories Papa told me that I remembered only because he told them to me so many times over the years:

> You are not here, you are here—
> in the vastness of the ocean
> you crossed, here
> in the house you called home
> for nearly 50 years.

Here in the stories you told
time and time again:
How when you met Mama,
she pretended not to notice,
stealing glances from behind
a comic book;
How you eloped on leap year and
swore you didn't realize
you wouldn't have to give
an anniversary gift but
every four years;
How as a boy you had fangs for teeth?
And how—boom! They fell out at
the clap of hands by the medicine man;
How grandma taught you a little ditty:
"Oh, look at the moon; she's shining up there
Oh, how she looks like a lamp in the air."
I will think of you each time
I see a full moon—
Your face wide, eyes shining,
Smiling.

That line, "I will think of you each time I see a full moon" is a bit of a stretch, but I will try and remember my promise. I stare at the white stars on the flag that sits on Little Brother's lap. I will be taking the flag to my home in Texas, stow it on top of my treasure chests of memorabilia in the office closet until I remember to buy a case to enclose it. I may remember to place it atop the piano he bought for me soon after Mama died, which I plan on having shipped for a total of 1200 dollars, more than the piano is now currently worth. But that's okay, Papa left plenty enough to cover the funeral expenses and a 30%

share of the inheritance for me.

When the flower tribute—the last part of the graveyard service—is over, and all the guests are gone except for me, Little Brother, Big Sis and her family, I need a moment alone with Papa. I step onto the precipice and make the mistake again of looking down into the disinterred grave. I whisper Goodbye Papa, I love you. With no tissue or handkerchief, I must swallow my tears, cough, and wipe my nose with my hand. How many times have I already said goodbye—once when he died, again at the mortuary when I wasn't going to look but then did? Before falling asleep, and then again in the dark morning? This goodbye is different from the rest; it is the last time before Papa is buried forever. Soon, like Mama, he will be protected from the decomposing elements by a hard, cold, slab of concrete. My last glance down is not enough to bring up vivid memories of Mama. A vague sensation looms in the air because I am vaguely aware that Mama is buried deep— deeper in the ground below. I weep—not for Mama, but over the fresh loss of my father. I weep also over the fact that eventually I will feel little, if anything at all, when thinking of either of my parents, buried here, one on top of the other, one headstone stating something I no longer believe, and the other which will state the simple fact that my father served in the military and lived for 84 years.

*

Big Sis arrives in a smart black dress suit and heels, the ones she wears to special Jehovah's Witness events that happen only once a year, such as the Memorial of Christ's death. Her jet-black hair sits in a loose bun, the way she always wears it. I hug her, whispering, *You look beautiful*, in her ear. She steps down the inclined hill, and when I ask if she's okay, she sniffles back her tears and answers, *No, I'm not okay*. She hugs a bouquet of multi-colored roses close to her chest.

She makes a beeline to Mama's tombstone, etched with words of my creation so long ago, some twenty years now isn't it, when I was still a Jehovah's Witness—it's a shame she no longer is, Big Sis must be thinking. *How do you do it—face the world and death without any hope.*

Papa died at home, so he got his wish. Plus, he lived a long life. That and the fact that he's no longer in pain should console. And the resurrection, of course. Of course? But he died an unbeliever, so...

She sits in the front row on the left, next to her husband who sits on the aisle seat. She puts the iPad on the seat to her right so that Other Big Sis and family can observe the memorial service virtually. She gets her cue from the director, "And I think it's been touched upon, till we see each other again. Can I have two family members perform the flower tribute?"

I wave my hand, and she follows suit. She grabs my hand, and together we approach the threshold. She takes hold of the left side of the wreath while I grab the right. She sniffles back tears when she sees me trembling and sobbing uncontrollably. No need to grieve, she must tell herself, for Papa is at peace now.

When the flower tribute is over, Big Sis will forget everything the director said because her focus is on getting through this most painful loss of our last parent. I had to stop recording on my smartphone to participate in the tribute, and Big Sis's iPad served as a virtual window to real-time, not as a recording device. She will also forget because she must have said a silent prayer partly addressed to Jah—*Oh Jehovah, help me, help me let go—and partly to Papa, Forgive me.*

Not a burden to his children. Papa died on Wednesday morning at 3:41 in the presence of me and the hospice nurse on duty. At the time, Big Sis was asleep at home, but had her phone on. She had been on-call essentially for months, taking care of Papa as the only one of us living close by. On Monday night, when he was awaiting the oxygen machine and pain medication, he practically begged her to stay overnight, "But Papa," she said, "I can't. I'm so exhausted, and I must work tomorrow. If I don't go into work, I'll lose my job. Good thing I didn't stay and call in the next day," she explained later to me and Little Brother when she treated us to dinner at her favorite Chinese restaurant, very close to hers and to Papa's home. We hadn't asked her about that night, but she explained anyway. "Come to find out, as a part time teller at the bank, I don't qualify for FMLA."

She had tried to console him that her husband, his son-in-law that he loved, would stay with him. "Please, I'm begging you, understand. I'm about to pass out."

According to the scriptures, it is the grown children's God-given responsibility to care for their aged or aging parents. It would be a sin to neglect this duty. She is reassured from the outside that she did her best. After Big Sis explains herself at dinner, I remind her of how Papa repeatedly said, "I don't know what I would do without your sister. She has changed. She is so kind and does everything I ask of her." Yes, she got past old grudges over past injuries—both Papa and Mama not helping her when she broke out with the worst acne, Papa beating her legs with the vacuum cleaner that one and only time he lost his temper on her, and other regrets. Her selfless acts can partly be attributed to character, partly to religious conviction, partly out of genuine love for family. She carried the burden for almost two years. She visited him at least twice a week, bought his groceries for him, cooked meals, took him to the doctor, sat and talked. It had gotten very difficult in the past weeks. His left leg swelled so much it caused him great pain. She trimmed his toenails and what was left of his hair. But there were some things she was not trained for, such as helping him catheter (he wouldn't have let her even try anyhow). Finally, at the end, through a conference call, we convinced Papa that he needed hospice nurses to come and assist around the clock. We knew he was in a bad way when he acquiesced and agreed not only to the nurse assistance but to pain medication and oxygen. Big Sis remembers, for its still fresh, how pathetic Papa looked, slouched in his wheelchair in the kitchen, barely able to speak or to stay awake, asking when the oxygen would arrive. Will it arrive soon? It didn't get there until past 9 pm that Monday night, but when it did, she was relieved to see that it did give him some relief.

When Papa begged her to stay the night—this is something Big Sis won't and cannot ever forget. It was either stay with him till his last breath or lose her job at the bank, which she already nearly lost when our sister was dying from lung cancer four years prior and she had taken on the job of primary caretaker. She'll never know if she really would have lost her job had she stayed the night, if she would either have went to work without sleep and plowed through, or missed work and explained later that her one and only father was dying, he needed her, and her boss would have understood.

When I asked Big Sis to contribute a memory for the poem, Big Sis said, "I know Papa called you Baby, but did you know that I was his first Baby? You may be Papa's Baby, but I was the first."

"Yes," I said, "I know. He also said you were his Princess. You look beautiful. I wish Papa could see how you did this all for him."

Little Brother carries on his daily routine: Write at the coffee shop or library, pack a lunch of peanut butter and jelly sandwich, a bag of fruit or nuts, and a cannister of water to consume outside of the cafe or library, then resume work for a few more hours after, then get a more substantial dinner. "Everyone processes their grief in their own way," I say, stating the obvious in my attempt to gauge his feelings. "Writing is my way of dealing...dealing with life," he says. Onward then, for what can he do otherwise? We knew it was coming. Papa had been officially diagnosed with prostate cancer a year and a half ago, and most likely had it for several years prior, for he knew something was wrong but refused to be touched by anyone, especially by a doctor. Little Brother stops short of accusing Papa of letting himself die. For that was what we think anyway, we just don't say it out loud. "Still, you're never really prepared," I say. But Papa was. Papa had appointed me as Executor and Little Brother as co-executor, jobs neither of us wanted. "I'm smart on an intellectual, academic level," he insisted, but not with matters of daily affairs or red tape, that I hate." He will do his part, clean up the kitchen and toolshed, get it all done by himself in two days rather than taking staggered trips to Goodwill. Push through, keep busy with work. Death is inevitable, happens to us all. "I'm not one for rituals," he adds. "Being raised a Jehovah's Witness—you know how they shun rituals for the most part—has left its mark." Writing is a project of passion and he will not let anything get in the way. Besides, there'll be a time to grieve, he'll grieve in his own way. He has nothing to prove to anyone.

In reading Todd May's "A Fragile Life: Accepting Our Vulnerability," on the recommendation of Little Brother who used the book in teaching philosophy to his undergraduates, I am drawn to the stoic's acceptance of death, death as both tragedy and necessity. In "Death," a book by the same author, he expands on his argument that while death is an evil, so too is the notion of immortality. But none of what I read could prepare me for the visceral experience of seeing Papa's body one last time at the mortuary. I had decided I wasn't going to go in, that I wanted to remember him as he was, but that in itself was self-deceiving, for I had seen him die before my eyes and then rolled on the gurney into the vehicle that took him away from his home of 50 years. Other Big Sis had said, "You guys should go see, he looks better than I expected. He looks like he's at peace." So, I went in, he was dressed in a hospital gown, cold from refrigeration, and yes, he looked better than those hours right after he passed. Finally, not suffering anymore. *No more pain, Papa, no more pain.*

Now that the hardest part is over (or is it?), we must clear out as much as we can while here and after discussing with my siblings, I must make the final decision about what to do with the house. I could stay in the master bedroom, which has its own bathroom, but prefer to sleep in the blow-up bed in my old bedroom. I cannot bring myself to sleep in the same room where I witnessed Mama slowly deteriorate from cancer some 20 years earlier. A visitor peddling some nonsense "sound therapy" as a possible cure for late stage uterine cancer asked her if she wanted to live, to which Mama had nodded yes. Mama's pale, ghostly face, reminded me of the *Scream*. Out of that face came a strained plea to go on living. Yes, the drawn face said, I'll submit to any unproven method of therapy.

When clearing out the room, to my surprise, I found Mama's old brown and furry bed spread. The blood stain. I hadn't thought of any of this for years now, but the dried blood—Mama had coughed up blood, which at first, we thought was the grape juice she had just sipped. The blood seeped through the thick fur into the back side and the stain was still visible. I ask Big Brother to dump it with the rest of the trash, and he does. Papa stowed the blanket along with several other old sheets all these years. Neither of us comment on the obvious. Papa should have washed it if not thrown it out. Mama should have gone to the hospital the night before when everything hurt except her eyelashes. She wanted to spend one more night at home. "I love you, now let me go." I did not get to see Mama take her last breath but kissed her forehead and said goodbye in the cold hospital room where they moved Mama's body onto a cold steel bed. The dead need no comfort. I was the only one of my siblings who got to see Papa take his last breath but had arrived from the plane too late to speak to him while he was still conscious.

Writing is a way of handling life. I post about Papa's death on my blog the day before Christmas. I share the entry on Facebook and friends make comments such as "Beautiful words in the midst of grief," and "Very Moving." After revising and fine-tuning, I post an update: *I finished this piece...I think:*

Papa and Mama died 20 years apart. Mama died in 1998 and Papa in 2018. Mama in October, Papa in December, both near year's end.

I was born in 1969, which means Mama died when I was 29, so would not see me turn 30, and Papa died when I'm 49, so will not see me turn 50 in two months. Both died when I was on the verge of something—what some would call a landmark event. Or a new beginning.

The piano movers picked up the Young Chang upright piano Papa bought me in either 1999 or 2000. I'm afraid I don't remember the exact year, just that it was not long after Mama died, but I tend to think the gesture was partly out of tenderness and partly out of grief. For I reminded him of Mama, he often said, he called me Baby, a term of endearment much as he was lovingly called Boy, all his life by his siblings in the Philippines.

Moving the piano from his house in San Diego to Austin will cost 1200 dollars, probably more than the twenty-year-old piano is now worth. I looked up the year the piano was built using its serial number, and discovered it was built the same year Mama died, 1998. I'm not sure what this all means, but I'm compelled to force connections or to find patterns in matters beyond my control, so that I can find a commonality in my grief.

They both died from cancer, their deaths left me parentless. It feels as if Papa's death hits harder, but only because his death is fresh, and I have lived a greater portion of my life with him in it than without.

I will miss—

- calling you at least once a week, hearing you say, "I'm okay," when clearly you are not, and then turning the attention away from yourself to the other, "give my love to the other half."
- hearing the concern in your voice when you say, "Take care of yourself" and "your health is your capital." You worried about us girls because so far, the women in our family, Mama and Middle Sister, both died from cancer.
- the way you'd get lost in memory, your eyes losing their present focus, seeing hazy images of things long past, caked with grime and dust.
- how you would eat in silence at your favorite restaurant, Zorba's, savoring your food slowly and with care. This memory pains me now as I clear out the kitchen cabinets, throw out the unopened bottles of Ensure, half-eaten micro-waveable meals. Dozens of frozen single Sara Lee cheesecakes remain in the freezer and some in the vegetable bin. You told us many months ago that you couldn't taste food and had to force yourself to eat. The signs were there, but you kept going on while we were beside ourselves with worry, on call, phones never shut off, knowing one day soon we'd get the phone call. You'd pour salt on already sodium-rich food to make it palatable. You went from a robust weight to less than 120 pounds, from high blood pressure, to no pressure at all. The gasping for breath, wagging of the tongue in your final moments. Dressed in diapers, secreting

liquids that had to be sucked from your mouth, into a tube, then into a canister. The sight of unused packages of adult diapers makes me so sad, yet it all comes together like identical bookends, a cycle of birth and death. You used to say life was too short and you aimed for age 120. We used to say that you'd probably outlive us all, considering your strength and your stubborn will to live. Each birthday, your ritual was to read the number of the Psalms that matched your age to show gratitude for having lived that long. You were once a baby gasping for air, wailing and screaming in your first few moments in this world, and you went out gasping for air but keeping your cries to yourself. Somehow, despite the pain and sadness, it seems like this is how it's supposed to be. Death--both a friend and an enemy.

I don't know what all this really means, only that I wish to both forget and to not forget the terrible thing I witnessed: I, alone of all your children, saw your last gasps for breath, your last sigh I could have sworn was a call for my name, but couldn't have been—was your last breath an inward or outward breath? You said you didn't know how much time you had left, but that you were ready, you lived a long life. Were you really ready? Did you feel alone? Were you afraid? Did you hope to see Mama? Is she there with you? You are buried on top of her, just as you wished, and you died at home. Was that a comfort as you slipped away into unconsciousness? They said you could hear me, but could you really? No, really? Already some days have passed that I haven't thought much about you. I'm afraid--To forget seems to mean to move on and seems to equate to erasure, which in turn means I too shall one day be forgotten and erased. And I'm not ready, not yet, until I am. And then...

When I read my Ode to Death again, I see it as a vain attempt at coping, and worse, as maybe an exploitation of what should be private feeling. Yet again, and—it's true isn't it, the saying about time and distance...I am not as obsessed to relive my experience of his last breath or to know with certainty how he felt with none of his children right there to hold his hand before falling into unconsciousness...

A month after Papa's death, me and Big Sis exchange texts:

"Hey sis, how are you feeling?"

"I feel down a lot."

"Me too. I'm missing him a lot lately. So used to calling him I nearly did yesterday."

"Aww...yeah...sometimes I'm still in disbelief but, I haven't had what you call a meltdown yet cuz I've been staying busy. I was thinking...Maybe subconsciously I thought if I had some of sentimental things belonging to Papa or Mama it would ease the pain....... but no, nothing does."

Before my flight home, I tell Big Sis that I will call or text once a week to make sure she's okay. I know it will be especially hard for Big Sis, who must have gotten used to being Papa's primary caretaker of all his surviving children. As time goes on, I will forget my promise, not willfully. That's just the way it goes.

It is true, isn't it, what they say—who says? —that time and distance loosens the grip of grief...Where are the voicemails...did I delete them by mistake? Oh, God. Here they are. Good thing these texts I thought were deleted are not completely deleted. And I can save them forever if I want. Where is the voicemail my brother-in-law left, was it the day I flew out, the day Papa died, did he know I was coming? Is it too late to ask if brother-in-law told Papa I was flying in that day he fell in the bathroom, before he went comatose? Did he know his Baby would be there and so held on? *I'm sorry, Papa, I didn't come sooner, to be able to say goodbye.*

[10/28/18 0:25] "Hey Baby, it's Papa, I'm returning your call as I promised. So, I don't know where you're at now, but anyways, you give me a call if you have the chance. I love you Baby. Okay, bye."

SCHEMAS

Where do I begin? When did this madness begin to envelop me? Was it the antagonistic Denny's waitress, the aggressive bank teller, the dog and cat humping in the park, or catching Billy jacking off on *Playboy?* Somewhere in the provisional instants of time we call memories lies the epicenter of the tremulous ripples that sent me over the edge.

Astronomy 101. When I arrived late to class, I chose the metal chair in the back row, scooting it back to make room for my lanky legs. I rested my heavy backpack on my outstretched legs, forcing my battered heels against the floor. When Professor Astronomy flung the door open, sliding across the shiny, waxed floor that matched the bald spot on the top of his head, he was wearing the same tired t-shirt with the glow-in-the-dark planets and stars. I hated that shirt and the manner he took in his lectures, holding his skinny frame erect like a drill sergeant, seeing right through us as if we were transparent. He paused to place his briefcase on the table, tied the sparse strands of the tail of his ridiculous gray mullet into a ponytail, and pressed the button to lower the film screen.

The lights dimmed and the chapter on lunar eclipses appeared. I reached down for my study guide, and when I looked up, this is what I saw in glittering PowerPoint letters, appearing sequentially on the screen:

Y-O-U L-I-G-H-T U-P M-Y L-I-F-E

"It's karaoke time and we'll begin with my favorite, an oldie for you guys, not for me." He started belting out lyrics about having the hope to carry on, in a crackly, falsetto voice. I looked around at my classmates; they began blurring in the foreground. Fellow Student's head was tilted back, his mouth hanging wide open. "It breaks the routine, yeah?" I turned away and felt my own face contort into disbelieving expressions.

Professor Astronomy raced up the steps, the nostrils of his long, pointed nose flaring like a dragon, and lunged at Fellow Student, knocking him to the ground. "Drop and give me fifty," he ordered. "And you, Young College Student, put this on," he said to me as he pulled off his tired shirt and handed it to me. The ripples of his ribcage were showing, and I shut my eyes, but obeyed. Fellow Student counted, "Uno, dos, tres..." as he clapped his hands in between.

I ran towards the back exit, not daring to look back. I nearly turned back, hoping to see Professor teaching as usual, pointing to the phases of the moon with his laser pointer—no matter how boring – pausing for questions. It was the questions that led to thoughtful speculations, and to more questions, which led to answers that at least made sense. But this—none of this belonged to any familiar framework in my head.

But this isn't where it began. Somewhere in these past two weeks, something must have been the trigger. By this time in class, my pasty skin needed washing, white flakes drifting from my itchy scalp, and I was wearing the same white shirt sullied from over-wear. I restlessly rubbed at the stubble growing on my chin. I liked the scratchy feel on my fingertips, but not the hot row of acne bumps rising upon my left cheek. I felt dirty. I hadn't slept much, and my life had already taken a turn into uncertainty, I'm certain.

Maybe it was Sunday breakfast at Denny's, the weekend before Astronomy 101.

Everything had begun as usual – the hostess leading me to a comfortable booth by the window, handing me the breakfast menu: "Your waitress will be with you shortly." I tossed the menu aside and ordered my usual—the Grand Slam for $3.99. A new waitress walked towards my table, sliding into the booth right next to me, setting the iced water down. I looked at her lapel, which read, "Slam me!"

"How's it goin'?" she asked.

"I'm fine I guess," I answered, scooting closer to the wall. "You're new here?" I said, clearing my throat.

"Slammy, slamoo, slam you!" she jingled. "Your hair looks like it's on fire!" She must have noticed the red I had Billy add to the tips of my blazing black hair. "And what are your plans for the weekend?" she asked as she scooted closer to me, planting me against the wall. I sat in uncomfortable silence, staring down at her apron pocket, hoping she would get up and take my order. Instead, her eyes rolled around, back and forth. "Goshitsbeen-aroughweekforme-I'vebeenonmyfeet-twentyfourseven-andimtiredofallthegriping." After each syncopated phrase, she sucked in air. I whirled around, looking for help. She stood up and lit a cigarette.

"Hey," I whispered, "there's no smoking inside." She swept the cigarette from her lips with two fingers and ground it into my right hand. I yelped in anguish, splashing the cold water onto my hand. Then I splashed the rest in her face as I pushed her aside and made for the exit. Her voice trailed off as she announced, "The pie of the month is..."

I suppose I could've run back in and complained to the

manager, but I didn't. Act now, ask questions later. That's my way. So, this must've been it. This was the first of the many strange events of the last two weeks, which pulled the rug from under me, and swept me into a world unknown and unfamiliar.

When I left Denny's all I could think of was how I needed more cash. So, I drove to the ATM and punched my pin number in: 4, 2, 1, 6. That didn't work. I tried, 4, 1, 2, 6. That wasn't it either. Was it 4, 6, 2, 1? I was blocked out of the machine. It spit out my card, so I went inside the bank.

"Next member please."

"Well, this is embarrassing, but I forgot my pin number and can't get any cash from the ATM. Can I withdraw forty dollars please?"

"Certainly sir," the male teller answered. I didn't like being called sir, but I found his tousled brown curls attractive, and his Adam's apple rippling up and down as he spoke. "It happens more than you would think sir. Just fill out this form." It was odd that he was calling me sir, as I was still a young college student.

"Yeah, it's pretty humorous actually," I said un-sir-like. "This has never happened before."

"Sir just sign here please," he continued, annoying me despite the flash of his amazing blue eyes. "If you still can't remember your code later, just go to the customer relations desk and they will assist you in obtaining a new one." His manner was cordial, but uptight.

"Thanks, but I'm sure it will come back to me."

Yank. He pulled me by the collar and stuck his tongue in my mouth. I nearly choked, but the swirling of his tongue enthralled me, and he began sucking on my bottom lip. My heart beat rapidly as I both pulled away and drew into him. He tightened his grip and I succumbed. But then just as easily he let go, and I collapsed to the floor. I edged backwards like a crab, sweating, and watched the teller as he carried on: "Next member please."

Managing to hobble back onto my feet, I couldn't look up, out of shame. I felt for my lower lip but could only feel my fingertips. Trickles of sweat were blinding me as I struggled to the door. In the chaos of my mind, I could not remember where I had parked.

But despite the madness of these events, it was Billy. Billy sent me over the edge. Catching Billy just this afternoon in his bedroom, with the Summer Special Issue of *Playboy* in his hands. In one hand he held the magazine, and with the other, he was jacking off through the slit of his red-checkered under-shorts. I had gone into the kitchen a few minutes before to heat up rolled tacos in the microwave, and when I shoved the door open with my foot, I saw him yanking, pulling, his face squeezed like a prune. I shut the door without a word, laid the plate of tacos on the coffee table, and walked out the door.

As I sat down in my car, sighing heavily, struggling to catch my breath, I felt a tingling sensation down my legs before they went numb. I felt the urge to climb back into the warmth of Mother's womb, to call out to her for help. But she didn't know about Billy and me. At least I didn't think so. And even if she did, what would she say? Would she be accepting? Instead of comforting me, she'd accuse me of abandoning her just like Dad did years ago. Ever since then, I've been her sense of security, the man of the house...

Maybe she suspected, that night a year ago when Billy

and I first started seeing each other. That night we took a drive around downtown to spend some time alone. I kept my cell phone on silent, not even vibrate so I wouldn't feel it like a stun gun in my pocket through the night. Mom would always have some excuse to call, to remind me that we hadn't watched the rented videos yet that were due the next day, or that her home-cooked meal was waiting for me, getting cold. I didn't have a curfew anymore, but she always found some way to make me feel guilty that she was home alone again.

Billy drove that night, and when he dropped me off, he did so one or two houses away from mine, at my urging, just in case Mom was peeking through the blinds again. "Why do you worry so much?" he asked me, "She knows we're friends. You have friends." It was true perhaps that I was being paranoid, but I didn't want to make her suspicious. Billy and I had started off as friends. But then his common, small brown eyes grew uncommon to me. Deep and reassuring, they had a way of smiling at my eternally alarmed wide ones. Maybe Mom would catch on to this, a look passing between us. She's clairvoyant, Mom, with the uncanny ability to decipher the simplest expressions.

I wanted to spend the night with Billy at his place that night, but I knew that at eighteen years old, a sleepover would seem strange. And as I walked up my driveway, there was Mom, peeking through a small slit through the curtains. "That's odd," she said when I unlocked the door, "it's as if you just suddenly appeared. And your hair is all ruffled." I glanced at the round mirror hanging behind the door, and my normally perfect side part had indeed disappeared under disheveled tufts of overgrown hair.

"You didn't walk home did you?"

"No Mom, of course not," I answered. I couldn't lie to her and told her I had hung out with Billy. "Hmmmm," she said, with a meditative look. I looked away, making sure she couldn't study my face.

When I left Billy to his *Playboy,* I was tempted to go back inside, to give him a chance to explain. But my desire for Mom's warmth took over, and so I drove home.

It was dark, and after passing through the swinging wooden gate, I tried unlocking the door, but it was already unlocked. Strange, I thought. The fluorescent light didn't activate as usual, meaning Mom had not switched it on. She wasn't in the kitchen, and no food was on the table, covered and kept warm, waiting for me. The dishes were piled up in the sink. I tiptoed to check if there was any light coming through the slit under her bedroom door. It was dark. I heard mumbling from the living room, the flicker of lights calling to me in the darkness. I saw her sprawled on the couch, dozing in front of the television set. "Mom, it's me. Mom, what's for dinner?" I asked. She flinched and opened her eyes. She gave me a quick look over and turned her eyes back onto the T.V. screen. "That's not your shirt, is it." It was a statement, not a question.

"No Mom, it's not mine."

"Is it Billy's?" My heart beat rapidly again just as it did in the bank. Only it was out of fear rather than desire. Her voice was sleepy, icy and cold. I refused to answer that foreign tone coming from a familiar form. I made my way to the couch she lay upon and squeezed myself into the corner and against the armrest.

"You're a fag, aren't you? You and Billy."

I looked over at her. Her freshly black-dyed hair was

pulled back in a tight ponytail, rather than falling loosely onto her shoulders as it usually did. It made her slanted eyes look even narrower. She was wearing her terry white robe, the one I remembered from childhood, still soft and white like lamb's wool. She looked as if she had shrunk. But she wasn't old enough to shrink like old people do. I wanted to shrink, lie safely on her shoulder or back like I used to when I was a small child, while she watched her favorite shows from the corner of her eye. She hadn't really been watching, those lazy afternoons, but lulled into sleep by the constant streaming sounds. And I was lulled too, by the rise and fall of her breathing. I rode safely into those sweet dreams of flying in a rainbow sky or floating in the air. I could never remember waking up.

"God made Adam and Eve, not Adam and Steve," she continued. "If everyone were gay, that would mean the end of the human race. Then what about natural selection, survival of the fittest? There would be nothing fit to survive. There's a frozen Hungry Jack in the freezer."

As I sit here, I don't know how many hours have passed. Mom still lies there in the same position, her eyes now shut. The television is no longer hazy, and scenes from the ten-o'clock news are flashing, one after the other. The shadows and colors on the screen palpitate and pulse, mimicking the electrical pulses of my unstable heart.

Mother, you are the center of my madness. But the chill in the room is beginning to settle into my skin, melting into recognizable warmth. The right words will surely form on my tongue, and finally release. Everything that has taken me by surprise will, like all things, become used and familiar. A frozen Hungry Jack doesn't sound so bad after all.

FETISH (UNDER THE ACORN TREE)

He buried her braids
left them that way—
relieved of rubber bands and ribbons
then planted a tree
and let the acorns fall free

He never shed a tear
when speaking of her pain
only stretched one band—
a red one
to the spread of two fingers

It snapped at the last
right out the window
and he's been searching
for it ever since
among the weeds
and under the acorn tree

FETISH[1]

---

[1] In Slavoj Zizek's book, In Defense of Lost Causes, he illustrates fetish as that "which enables you to (pretend to) accept reality 'the way it is,'" by re-telling a story told in psychiatric circles "about a man whose wife was diagnosed with acute breast cancer and who died three months later." Here is the rest of the story: "the husband survived her death unscathed, being able to talk coolly about his traumatic last moments with her-how? Was he a cold, distant, and unfeeling monster? Soon, his friends noticed that, while talking about his deceased wife, he always held a hamster in his hands, her pet object and now his fetish, the embodied disavowal of her death. No wonder that, when, a couple of months later, the hamster died, the man broke down and had to be hospitalized for a long period, treated for acute depression." Now this nonfiction version of the story of the fetish might strike you as more interesting than the poetic version above. Perhaps – but allow me to explain my choice of a rubber band as the physical fetishistic object of the character (or more accurately – the "voice" of the poem). I've already used a non-fiction reference to a hamster for the purpose of metaphor in my published work, "God is in the Ceiling," wherein I include a real-life incident of my pet hamster's death, which I thought at the time was instigated by my sister Dyna. Certainly there is no rule against using the same object/metaphor in more than one creative piece, but I felt the need for the use of fresh imagery for this particular piece, and as far as I can recall, I've not previously used the image of a stretched, therefore tensed rubber band, nor any reference to acorn trees in previous work. Weaving the two unlikely and dis-connected objects so closely together in the above poem makes for a more provocative, engaging fictional illustration of fetish than the more predictable, albeit realistic anecdote of a troubled man and his affection for his dead wife's pet.

GOD IS IN THE CEILING

My sister said that when you sleep on the top bunk, you're closer to God. And so we switched places, despite my fear of heights. The ladder, she told me, would prevent me from falling off in the middle of the night.

My sister killed my hamster.

*

Certainly, one can die by being killed. But killing is not really about death, which is dormant and passive. Killing is about power and control.

She said I'm the source of her infection. All I did was finger her. My fingers were sullied with incense.

*

I don't want you anymore. Not now. For sure, not tomorrow. Yes, there was a time when you were very young (you're still young), and just the way it felt having your tongue swirl around, the way my b-size fit snuggly into your c-shaped mouth.

But now I watch you, slouching in that chair, the tips of your boots touching the tips of my toes, and I feel nothing. You are here, yes, but already you are filed away in the appendix of my mind I will visit upon only at the end, when I've forgotten the order and the matter.

*

I don't use incense in the religious sense. I use it to clear my sinuses. And to make my fingers smell like something other than cigarettes. One needs to clear the senses from time to time.

Shove fingers in and out. Pull hair. Twist and bite.

*

When I was a little girl, I used to think God was in the ceiling. And so I slept close to him. I searched for him in the dark. My sister told me that if I stared long enough and hard enough that eventually I'd see him.

God seemed to oversee everything. *God damn you! So help me God! God damn it!* Who was God?

Night after night I stared at the ceiling. I saw Colonel Sanders, or maybe it was Santa Claus. I saw bunnies and stars and crossword puzzles. I saw letters and numbers, and spots. Finally, I saw what had always been there—a ceiling with lots and lots of bumps. I didn't get upset or accuse my sister of playing a trick on me. I had faith. And I didn't blame God because, after all, he had enough on his hands. How could he bother showing himself to a curious little girl who had already seen too many things?

I knew God would one day show himself to me, when I was good and ready.

*

I like sex. A lot. But I get infections. A lot. Is God trying to tell me something?

I'm not the only one obsessed with God. *Children of a Lesser God. The God of Small Things. God is watching us.*

Tell me all your thoughts on God, 'cause I'd really like to meet her...

Back to sex.

God is dead. Now, for that statement to carry the weight that it does means that God had to have been at some point, kind of a big deal.

And now God is dead, everywhere and all around me.

*

Keep it simple:

- Turn out the lights.
- Light a candle. And incense.
- Listen.
- Toss a hard object against the mirror in the ceiling, just as she requests.
- One-hundredth crack in the mirror.
- Feel.
- Wiggle your fingers.
- Don't shove.
- Rub.
- Smoke a cigarette.
- Begin, all over again.

*

I'm happy now. But most of the time I'm not. Is that the way it is for everyone?

The orchids on my balcony are dying. I try to keep my plants alive but can't seem to do so. I read the directions for taking care of orchids, which said to water twice a week when it's hot and once a week when it's not. Do not overwater. They need direct sunlight. Pretty simple. I followed the directions to a T, and still my orchids are withering and dying.

Most of the time I feel a sense of fear. I don't know of what. And anger. I see and hear too many things at once.

One morning, I heard someone shouting, even with my window closed. The voice shouted: "Fuck your mama. Fuck your brother. Fuck the wind. Fuck that tree. Fuck the trolley. Fuck this shit!" Or something like this. I peeked through the window and to my surprise saw a well-dressed man. He wore a light-colored trench coat with a briefcase in one hand. He was clean-shaven and looked like he was headed to a corporate job. Just before he turned the corner, he added: "Get the fuck away from me and take Big Bird with you!"

That's what it's like. I look normal. I dress for the role. But inside my head is a slew of curse words and gibberish. I'll be carrying on a conversation with a friend over coffee, just as dozens of times before and note the barista working her fingers over the new computerized register. The loud whirring of the coffee machine. A whiff of vanilla or Brazilian beans. My partner's mouth moving, head cocked back. The picture frame behind his head crooked. A young couple simultaneously leaning over the counter. The barista taps and taps. Two white Macbooks open, side by side. The whirring stops and starts all over again. I've heard my friend's words but don't understand what he's said.

Fuck coffee. Fuck Mac. Fuck young love.

Does that make sense?

*

I remember once when I was a child (or was it a dream?) my mom was mad at me for some reason, and so she reached into my shorts and pinched my groin real hard. She didn't pinch my penis. Had she intended to and missed?

I still like sex. With her I just finger and kiss. My partner likes it if I don't aimlessly shove. And she makes me wash my hands because she's allergic to incense and cigarettes.

Does this make sense?

*

My therapist made me cry today. She proposed a new therapy for my anxiety: "It's called EMDR, which stands for Eye Movement...Desensitization...Let me see, I can't remember what the R stands for. Let me just go get the paper. That'll make it a lot easier."

She told me that oftentimes panic or anxiety attacks stem from a traumatic experience way back in one's childhood that one relives in the present. It is re-lived in the sense that you feel the same feelings you did when the trauma happened, minus the actual event. My heart started beating more rapidly as the thought occurred to me that maybe something traumatic had happened to me that I couldn't remember.

"There are eight phases to the treatment," she said, reading from a paper in her hand. Several seconds of silence passed as she scanned down the page before she read to me the first phase. "Sorry, my last client—that was really intense," she said, as if to excuse her absentmindedness. She continued, "Now I want you to think about the most recent emotionally disturbing event, and then come up with an image of it."

I imagined and said, "I remember when my sister pulled down my pants and then pulled down her own and said we should rub our butts on the bed. She then quickly pulled her pants back up and then told me to do the same."

The therapist eyed me carefully through her glasses and said, "Is that the most recent?"

"No. That was when I was eight," I answered. "But you know, my sister also killed my pet hamster. She hated the squeaky sound of the wheel in the middle of the night. She denied it of course...want me to think of a more recent trauma?"

The therapist nodded, and "And remember, don't recount the experience to me, just create a picture in your head that represents the event." I thought and thought and couldn't create an image, so I lied and said, "Okay, I have it."

In Phase Two, she must have been feeling me out as she asked me if I was okay and encouraged me to take a deep breath. And so I did. I felt lightheaded but didn't say so.

She then showed me a laminated list of negative feelings and asked me to identify one or two that this recent traumatic event made me feel. "I am unworthy and ashamed." I pointed at this one, even though I wasn't sure of what I was unworthy or ashamed. She then asked me to pinpoint on the opposite side of the page a preferred positive belief. This was too obvious: "I am worthy and deserving of love."

I was then asked to focus on the negative image that I had supposedly conjured up and at the same time the negative feelings that came with it, simultaneously moving my eyes back and forth following her fingers. The purpose of this was to allow new insights and associations to emerge, or to trigger a traumatic memory that reaches far back. She asked what distance felt most comfortable and at what speed. My eyes moved back and forth as she swept her fingers back and forth about midway between us, slowly from right to left, left to right. My heart beat faster and faster as I expected to witness an image of me being molested or raped at the age of five or six, or maybe even younger. Nothing. Maybe the memory was repressed too deep. Back and forth, left to right. Any moment now. She told me to just notice. Nothing. Back and forth, right to left.

"Is this distance okay?" she asked, as her hand moved a little closer to me. Maybe she thought I would panic if she got too close.

"Yes," I said.

"I'm not going too fast?"

"No, that's just right." I felt dizzy and nearly out of breath. Just let whatever happens happen. Scream if you feel like it. It would surface any second now. I don't know if I can handle this...

Nothing.

Her hand stopped.

"How do you feel?"

"I feel like crying."

On the drive home, I formulated a list in my head of missing memories:

No heart-to-heart talk about sex, with either of my

parents. No explanation for my first period. No explanation of why you had to get married first before having sex.

Memories of what was said:

God made man and woman. God made one man for one woman. When a man and a woman love each other, they marry each other and are bonded for life. Love is not love unless it lasts forever.

Memories of what was not said but understood:

Sex = Love. God oversees love; thereby he's in charge of sex. Don't make God blush.

The therapist had said to take a deep breath and release. And so I took a deep breath and released. Somehow, I felt like crying.

*

I'm not in love with him. But I love sex. Finger, rub, and kiss. This isn't sex. Sometimes you must sacrifice the things you love for other things you love.

I love lying side by side, holding hands, staring at the cracked mirror in the ceiling. I don't know what he sees, but I see disjointed parts of ourselves, mostly of myself as when your eyes are drawn to yourself in photos, no matter who else is in the photo—even your lover.

I don't expect this to turn into love because we don't have sex.

I reimagine many things. Mother banging brother's head against the kitchen tile. He had forgotten to clean his room. Because he was a boy, he had his own room.

The janitor at my school whacking a trapped hummingbird to death with a broom in our classroom. He could have just sat there and waited instead, with the windows and doors open.

Father crying with no tears coming out.

Our disjointed body parts are like pieces to a puzzle you can put back together in a variety of different ways. I like it better this way.

It's somehow soothing just knowing the parts are there in the mirror in the ceiling.

*

Truth or dare. Kill a snail. Either that, or admit I kissed dirty Jodie in the sandbox. I hit the snail with my bare fist, so swiftly it felt like I had killed nothing. Until bits of shell and mush oozed down the side of my hand. I lurched and wiped slug guts onto my pants. It couldn't have felt anything. Not like Tommy's snail. He said he boiled one alive once, but that it was no fun because it hid in its shell the whole time. Tommy wouldn't dare soil his hands and dirty his pants.

I don't know why I remembered that just now.

I like lying on the bed with her, staring up at the cracks in the mirror. I know it's probably not normal to keep a cracked mirror on the ceiling. And we'll have to take it down soon before it breaks into a million shards. She laughs and says that when we take down the mirror we might as well remove the roof as well. The night sky is great and vast and open.

*

So, let me see if I can get this straight:

Keep it simple.
Wash your hands before and after.
Go for therapy but note the effects.
God is in the ceiling.
In your head.
Is that right?
Yes, that's correct.
Simply put, yes.
Thank God.

NON-TOUCH

We lay on our backs topless, our faces turned to each other. Noses only inches apart. We stayed in this position for quite some time. He was the first to say it.

"I'm feeling a kink in my neck."

"Yeah, me too."

So, we shifted to our sides. We observed each other blink. I focused on his lazy eye. It was sexy the way his eyelid curved over the pupil, like a peepshow. I separated my lips, just enough to savor his hot breath. His tongue did a striptease, wagging and then rolling. My tongue mocked his. They never touched.

After some time passed, it became difficult to remain on our sides without falling into each other. And so, I thought up a brilliant idea. I asked him to lie on his back with his arms spread out and his legs closed tight. I then utilized my athletic arms and legs to hold my body right above his. I balanced my weight on my hands below his armpits and the balls of my feet around his ankles, bending my knees slightly for stability. The tips of my nipples nearly brushed his chest.

Neither of us spoke now. I thought of her, their bodies and tongues entwined. Him dragging her body down the sheets to thrust deeper. But this was all the better. This was something she would never have. My arms began to tremble, and I focused on the tip of his nose, the tiny flakes of dried skin and the tender pink underneath. Furry black coils peeked out of his nostrils. He crossed his eyes and I giggled. We shadow-rubbed our noses together. I felt aroused with every non-touch.

Before we could further explore the sensations of this position, my limbs began to shake, my body nearly caving in on top of his. I managed to swing my body over, landing on my back.

I purposefully licked my lips as he stared at me sideways. His lazy eye twitched, twice in a row. He was aroused. He then rubbed his reddened cheek and pondered.

He took nearly the same position as I had, suspended right above my body, his chest nearly touching my breasts. Only he kept his legs closed and balanced on his feet between my legs. As he remained steady in this position, I flapped my arms like wings and opened and closed my legs like scissors.

The nearness of his body proved too much for me. I stuck my tongue out, reaching for his lips. His eyes grew wide as I flapped my arms and opened and closed my legs faster.

The more he trembled, the more I reached until I managed to lick his lips. They tasted like salted Chapstick. His body gave way and he landed on top of me. I wanted to wrap my arms and legs around him, smothering first his mouth and then his chest with open mouth kisses. And then he would pull my hair back and suck on my neck.

He removed his inflamed body from mine. We were once again face to face. He shut his eyes, and his breath was cool and sweet. I watched him fall asleep.

If he had been sedated.

Or fickle.

Or weak.

I would have:

Traced the curve of his eyelid with the tip of my pointer

finger.

Licked his eyelashes, one eye at a time.

And then his chin. And then his cheek.

Aimed the tip of my right nipple into the hollow of his mouth.

Pressing it against his wet tongue.

But I won't have it.

BACKWARDS

Mother was taken away, not because she channeled Lot's wife through the saltshaker, but because she poured salt into her open wounds.

The pepper was Lot, the countertop Gomorrah. "It's fitting that Lot wear black," mother said, "for black is the color of mourning." The salt, Lot's wife, was spilled all over the white, sprinkled-with-green, kitchen countertop. "The green dots," she reasoned, "are the grains of sand still visible after God, the stainless-steel knife, turned Lot's wife into a pillar of salt."

I was eight years old. Mother had been reading Bible stories to me at bedtime from the time I was five. By this time, Father had been gone for several months. We were well beyond Genesis and into the second book of Chronicles. I wondered about Lot's daughters. How would we portray the part (after their mother's transformation into a heap of sodium) where they kept feeding their father wine and each in turn entered the cave and lay down with him? I didn't know Bible people could drink wine. And weren't Lot's daughters too big to sleep with their daddy in the same bed?

Mother's cheeks turned pink and then she said:

"Let's not get distracted from what we're doing here. We are putting ourselves in her shoes. We are re-living the looking back of Lot's wife."

"And God made it rain sulfur from the heavens upon Sodom and upon Gomorrah, for the weight of their sins was very heavy. Men lay with men, following the lusts of their hearts. He overthrew these cities, even the entire

District and all the inhabitants of the cities and the plants of the ground. And his wife began to look around from behind him, and she became a pillar of salt."

Only now do I realize that Mother tried to shelter me from Old Testament horrors. She sought to kill my incest curiosity and pique my interest in Lot's wife. Lot's wife was not a horror. The horror was her turning into salt. Mother said the only reason she hadn't turned into salt when father left was because she refused to look back. She forced herself to look forward to all the possibilities. This did not last long. I watched her turn the other direction. She would sit in the living room, watching TV or reading a book, all the while looking back at the front door. Staring back at the door failed to make it open. This was Mother. At that I wondered, why did Lot's wife look back?

The play was Mother's idea. We had both grown tired of simply reading the Biblical narrative and agreed we needed to see this extraordinary scene in action. After the stainless-steel knife knocked over the saltshaker, spilling heaps of salt all over the countertop, Mother licked salt from it several times before she rubbed the saltshaker like a Genie bottle. I expected to see some ghostly, shadowy figure rise from the shaker. Instead, Mother closed her eyes and chanted:

"Yes, I am Lot's wife. I am Lot's wife. But I don't have a name. No matter. I am merely an instrument of God, to be upheld as an example for all. He tells me to keep my eyes on the prize ahead of me beyond the valley, upon the unseen, which frightens me. Not back at the world behind me, lusting after the momentary attachments of this world. Don't look back at mere grains of sand in the wind."

When Mother finally opened her eyes, they were full

of longing. She glanced over her shoulder one more time. That's when God punished her. The stainless-steel knife began making cuts into her wrist. I watched with awe as she scooped salt into the wounds. When she stopped, her eyes froze like the cold, still swirls of beautiful marbles.

For a long time after, I tried to put all of this behind me. I refused to look back. I practiced strict discipline upon my memories. When one would creep up, I'd shove it back down. I tried envisioning a whole new future for myself, but with no memories it was like trying to build a tree house without a tree.

It wasn't long before I returned to these memories of Mother and of God (or they returned to me). The more I remembered God's cruelty, the more I wanted to defy him, even if it meant possibly incurring his wrath upon me.

I made it a practice to look back. In defiance of my own safety, I would look back in the middle of the crosswalk. In my backward gaze, I'd see mostly forward-looking faces, oblivious to what lingered behind them: A hand of a boy clasped tight by a mother. A cheek of a mother kissed by a father. A man with his arms wrapped around another man. *More than grains of sand, God. More than grains of sand.* I'd catch someone else turning back like me and wonder – *do you see what I see?* A little girl stumble and scrape her knee. An old man takes a misstep off the curb, helped right back on again. *More than just pedestrians.*

But looking back in the crosswalk was not enough. Day in, day out, I managed to cross safely. God's wrath had not come upon me. And so, I took up jogging backwards around the lake on Sundays. I jogged backwards and at the same time turned my head back to stare at all the pretty boys and all the pretty girls as they passed me. Sometimes, I would stop in my backward tracks and strike up a conversation with someone moving in the opposite direction. Not surprisingly, I was asked more than once why I jogged backwards. My response? Why do you jog forward?

I did everything I could think of backwards: I read the Bible completely from back to front and yet it all sounded the same to me. I turned back the hands of the grandfather clock every night in hopes of defying the hand of God, but every other clock remained on schedule the following morning—mocking me. I wore skirts, pants and hats—all of them—backwards, all with no backlash. God didn't give a damn, nobody complained, and so living backwards became automatic and routine, even leaving behind every boy and girl I'd meet.

One day, I looked at my face in the mirror, but it refused to look back at me. In its place gaped a hollow hole – a deep dark abyss, infinity of nothingness. After who knows how long of staring into that lifeless pit, something began to rise from out of it, mired in the heavy weight of yesterday. So heavy that it took everything to tear my eyes away. I took that mirror down, threw it away and haven't replaced it since.

All that's left of Lot's Wife is a mound of salt somewhere near the Dead Sea. All that's left of Mother are my memories. And here I am, still walking and jogging and doing my thing. Nothing really turns my head, unless it's something out of the ordinary—or extraordinary.

BECKETT AND WOOLF

They posed for the sake of the shoulder, saw it odd to stare straight and smile, waiting for the flash like we do these days. He might have combed his hair with his fingers first (his wavy white and gray). She might have smoothed her skirt (even though it would never appear). One cannot think of her own death when posing (or can she?) He probably got it right after the second try, she the first (her parted lips suggesting impatience). I want to wear my hair like hers (loose, uncoiling slowly throughout the day). I want to navigate the straits of his face into that wide foaming open. I want to see myself the way others would dream me and then look away.

PERFORMANCE ARTIST

"Dress in all off-white like the tint of the sand in the hourglass. Let hair hang loose and sweep it forward. Do makeup, as you like. Flip over the hourglass, hold still and repeat: specter, specter, specter, specter, specter, specter —stress on first syllable. Draw out the word until three-quarters of sand have passed, and then—and only then— flip over the hourglass again. Repeat four times."

This is the gist of the script.

Arthur's voice is a deep baritone. Not that it matters. The audience never hears him speak.

Arthur expects me to follow the details of his script to a T, but for me what he's asking for feels unnatural. I know, I know, I'm an actor, a performer. So stop complaining, you'll say. At any rate, I wish Arthur would give me freedom to interpret the performance my way.

As I write this performance piece, I think of specter. It won't let me be. I sit here and just think. I move, but specter doesn't. It repeats in the same position. Why not 'ghost' rather than specter? Specter gives pause. Then repetition. That's it, repetition, ignorant of time. Mesmerize with the repetition of specter, specter, then snap the audience into consciousness of time. Hourglass as metaphor, eyes and ears transfixed until everything falls away except for silence, sand, and specter.

Arthur's speech is slow. He walks with both hands in his pockets, and his shoulders meet his ears. That's all I really know about Arthur, aside from his script.

Where have I seen 'specter'? Why does it repeat over and over in my head? Specter calls to me for a reason. Must appeal to the audience, give them a reason to respond to specter as I do.

I asked Arthur why he doesn't just perform this piece himself. I told him he has the voice for it. He says he's a writer, not an actor or performer. True, but considering that most of this performance requires movements rather than words, I'm sure he could carry it out just as well as me. He just shrugged and said nothing. A man of few words.

*

The audience clapped with enthusiasm between scenes and at the very end. You would think Arthur would be pleased, but he is not. Arthur blames me for doing things my way, for putting too much of my own style and energy into the performance, rather than allowing the performance piece to speak for itself. Though he hasn't said this, I'm sure this is what he thinks. Afterward, he said to me, "Please just perform the piece exactly as I've written it." What other way is there to interpret this?

*

Things are becoming complicated. Though technically I didn't alter anything, I performed Specter with my own interpretation tonight. What does 'specter' even mean? What exactly are Arthur intentions? There's only so much you can read into words on a page. You must go with your gut. All I know is that when I performed tonight, as I repeated the word *specter, specter,* I did so with a broken heart.

He must have caught on. After the performance, he didn't compliment my performance but just looked at me with a scowl. For him, it's all about his script. He cares nothing about the performer. Still, he knows very well he needs the performer just as much as the performer needs him, his script.

*

Despite everything, Arthur has kept me on as his Performance Artist. Tonight's audience was just as enthusiastic as all the others. This was probably just as successful (at least in my eyes) because I performed the piece my way, from that place within that cannot be replaced. No, I did not try to artificially bring back the feeling I had in previous performances. I went with what specter felt like tonight. What will specter feel like next time?

*

I've decided to confront Arthur. His name appears on the playbill of the performance, his and his alone. Clearly, this is giving misinformation at the least, withholding vital information at the most. I'm sure the audience will question things once they really think about it. They'll ask: 'Besides author, is Arthur also the performer? Like a singer who is his or her own lyricist?' Frankly, to me, the name "Arthur" suggests one thing and the performance another. If no one questions this then I wonder—can the audience not tell the difference between the true performer and the writer? Between the performance and the author of the script? I plan on asking Arthur to include my name on the playbill as the Performance Artist, even if my name should appear underneath his.

*

Arthur refuses to name me as the Performance Artist. One young lady came up to him after the last performance and asked for his autograph. When he signed his name, she stared down at the unreadable signature, turned to her friend and said admiringly, "Look! I got the Performance Artist's autograph!" and walked away utterly content.

I have decided to create my own performance. I will both write the script and perform it. I won't use the repetition of one word alone like Arthur does. I will use a unique arrangement of words. Or maybe I won't use any words at all.

*

I haven't kept up with the latest on Arthur. I don't know if he found someone else to perform for him, or if he has finally taken up his own performance.

I perform in complete silence now, letting my subtle movements project intense feeling. I allow them to maximize into grander gestures when called for, and to minimize to stillness at the end of it all.

My audience seems to recognize me by my performance, and my performance by me, just as it should be.

ARMS AND HANDS

Kyle said it was his hand that had pulled the trigger.

I held my boy on my lap, my arms embracing his. "Junior was this close to being hit," I said, failing to gesture with my hands.

"You should have seen the blood guzzle out of his head, like crude oil overflowing from a cracked pipe."

I covered Junior's ears. This wasn't supposed to be about Kyle's daddy.

"You know, the sensation that part of your body is not your own? There are people who swear by that feeling all their lives."

Yes, I remembered such a feeling—only once or twice —before realizing that it had just been a dream. That one time when I grabbed one hand with the other and threw it across the bed. It felt like I was grabbing someone else's hand that at the same time was my hand, so that when I woke up, I was surprised to find both hands still there.

I squinted at the walls of our living room, each one equally white and bright. The slits of daylight shining through the vertical blinds added nothing to the uninterrupted glare of the barren walls.

I wanted to escape the memories of Kyle's past, or the memories of his memories in my mind. He would blurt them out at odd times, generating uninvited images in my head. They did violence to me, so that I could feel the terror of a scream imploding, with no one else to hear, where even shutting my eyes felt unsafe.

"We really ought to hang some pictures up," I said softly, now rocking Junior with a loosened grip. I thought of family photos, with their eternal grins.

"Maybe you're right." Kyle grazed the top of my head with his hand as he passed towards the opposite wall, softly skimming its surface with his fingers. "But when I touch the naked wall like this, it feels so cool." Not like his daddy's fury. Daddy used to shout, stop making my blood boil.

I lifted Junior from under his arms, gently placing him on the floor. He held one arm out towards his daddy, stretched out straight, but limp at the wrist. Kyle failed to take his hand, just as he had failed that very morning. "He's still just a baby," I whispered, recalling the horror of the screeching tires and my body gripped in terror, as the car just missed him by inches. I thought that Kyle had him by the hand as they crossed the busy street intersection, while I trailed behind. But when I raised my eyes up, Kyle had his arms folded while Junior wobbled ahead.

Kyle stared at Junior's wrist, gripping his own tightly behind his back. "Wrists can be bent backwards or forward." He had told me in the past that when his daddy wasn't around, he would practice, to see how far he could bend them, to get them stronger and ready, for the next time.

"An arm can take on a life of its own."

And that's what he had told the court.

I watched Kyle as he stared at Junior arching his shoulders, swinging his arms freely.

He pushed back the black-rimmed glasses from his sweating nose, which failed to keep back the flames that seemed to flash from his eyes.

This was after all, about his daddy. Ignoring the sensation of panic rising within me, I asked. I had to be sure. "I know you've told me the story of that awful night before. But when your aunt testified in detail about what she saw your daddy do that night, was she right? Was it really that bad?" I asked, instantly recognizing the answer in the way Kyle Senior stood several feet away from Kyle Junior, stepping back further as Junior reached for him with his fingertips. I couldn't remember the last time he had picked up or held his son.

Together, we watched Junior lean forward, swinging his arms around in circles. And in that moment of unrestrained freedom I couldn't help but remember my own version of that violent night.

A young boy yanked off the bunk bed. Yanked by one arm and slammed into the floor.

One arm yanked. Body slammed against the floor.

Yanked by the arm. Body slammed.

Maybe the little boy saw his arm fly across the room after his face smashed against the hard wood floor. The arm was no longer his.

The movement of Junior's arms appeared random, prodding him clumsily forward. Kyle grabbed from under one arm, and then the other as my boy's feet shuffled off the floor. I cried out—from fright or relief—I'm still not sure.

AFTER-IMAGE

The cat purrs. A whistling sound comes from its nose. The woman lies in another room but can hear with her eyes closed. What she cannot hear is the soft padding of the cat's feet.

The man has been nearly deaf since age three. He turns down his hearing aid when he needs to think. For example, now in a loud bar, he nods his head while listening. He turns the dial down, inventing lines of rhyme and reasoning.

The cat is under the cabinet. She can tell by the jingling of its bells. It must be licking itself or stretching its feet. She chooses to listen to the bells rather than the people speaking on TV.

He sees a finger coil a curl, the snatch of an earlobe. That one smiling and laughing will have trouble sleeping. He can tell by the way her hands tremble while she's drinking. And how she looks away and stares into the ceiling.

I don't remember, she says, peering at one particular book on the nearby shelf. A book she once read some time ago. She pulls it from its place, lies back down, and begins reading. And it all comes back to her, as in a feeling.

He will memorize the bar scene like a movie script and remember it vividly, partly because he doesn't drink, mostly because he loves poetry. And then one day—for the life of him—he won't be able to recall the details, or the order in which they happened. He won't remember the reasons. When he goes to the bar again, he won't even notice the brand-new furniture or new drink offerings.

The names are new and so is her mood. The cat pounces on her lap. Unexpectedly. She scoots it off. It lands on its feet. She falls asleep. The cat returns and licks her cheek. She talks in her sleep. It nibbles on the last page read. Something about the beginning and the end.

WAKING HOURS (FICTION)

The cat—in play-dead position, marble eyes rolled back—murmurs like a dreamer. Maybe she is prey in some exciting chase. Maybe the fluttering of her eyes and the quivering of her mouth are merely a reflex.

The man who looks like a child sits on the floor, dressed in a sweater and tie. The documentary film camera focuses on him for a (painfully) long time. Both deaf and blind, he's forgotten how to speak and write. Incapable of dressing himself and maybe of abstract thinking. When he spits and drools and slaps his cheek, listen to what he is saying.

The philosopher threw himself out the window. Maybe death's delay was too much to take, and after years of deliberation he took the leap.

If you could pray, maybe you would ask to die a sudden death unexpectedly. Or maybe you would choose. Time to pay. Time to pay.

Do not be sad when death arrives, someone somewhere must have once said. Welcome and accept it, rather than crying like a lost child.

The man-child can't help it. He spits and dribbles. He winks.

The cat can't help sleeping through the waking hours.

There are worse things than death.

Hand the man-child a banana and he will eat immediately. He may never think of a tree the way a philosopher thinks of one, but he can feel one with his hands and climb it without analyzing what makes a tree a tree.

If the man-child could speak, maybe he would say: This constant buzzing in my head. Make it stop—please. If you do, I will stop slapping and scratching myself, stop crawling on all four of these things you call hands and feet.

The philosopher threw himself out the window. Suddenly. Maybe it was merely a reflex. Contradiction. After several years of struggling to breathe.

Look before you leap.

The philosopher starts from the position of thinking.

The cat stares for hours on end, when she's not sleeping. Maybe daydreaming. In between.

WAKING HOURS (ANTI-FICTION)

If a cat—or any other mammal for that matter—is observed murmuring, its eyes fluttering, and its mouth quivering, can it be claimed that it is dreaming?

Psychology Today claims that animals do in fact dream. Scientists are confident that all mammals dream. According to research conducted at MIT, "rats have been shown to dream about previously running a maze, and researchers have also discovered that they have complex dreams."

If rats can dream complexly, so can cats.

Of what exactly rats and cats dream, scientists are not sure. Some speculate that future researchers will find the answers. For now, one can only imagine: running a maze, pouncing, playing, prey in some exciting chase.

*

Werner Herzog's 1971 film *Land of Silence and Darkness* includes footage of Heinrich Fleischmann, a man both deaf and blind, who has forgotten how to speak and write, and has lived in a stable with animals. He stumbles into a tree, feeling the trunk and branches and leaves.

Footage of a man both deaf and blind, Heinrich Fleischmann, is included in the film *Land of Silence and Darkness.* Fleischmann has forgotten how to speak and write. At some point, he lived in a stable with animals. The camera focuses on him stumbling into a tree, feeling the trunk, branches, and leaves, among other things.

We see Heinrich Fleischmann sitting on the floor, appearing as a man-child, dressed in a sweater and tie. The camera seems to focus on him for a (painfully) long time. We see him eat a banana. We see him stumble into a tree, feeling the trunk and branches and leaves. Who wouldn't feel moved? If we are not moved, this says something, though what exactly one can't be completely certain.

*

OBITUARY: Gilles Deleuze

"—he committed suicide by throwing himself from his flat in Paris—"
Source: *The Independent* online archive, published Wednesday 08 November 1995.

"In 1995, he committed suicide, throwing himself from the window of his apartment."
Source: *Wikipedia.*

"November 4, 1995. Avenue Niel, Paris. The broken body of an old man lies crumpled on the footpath. It is that of Gilles Deleuze, the philosopher. His apartment room window, three stories above, stands open. There is no suicide note, yet it is clear enough what has happened. After twenty-five years of increasing physical infirmity, *the*

struggle to live had become too much for Deleuze and he took his life" (italics added).
Source: *First Things*, Issue Archive, May 2007.

First Things Masthead: "First Things is published by The Institute on Religion and Public Life, an interreligious nonpartisan research and education institute whose purpose is to advance a religiously informed public philosophy for the ordering of society."

Fact or fiction?

Google News: The Post and Courier—Nov 6, 1995, *Philosopher Gilles Deleuze commits suicide at 70*, Associated Press.

"The author of one of the world's best-selling philosophy books, "The Anti-Oedipus," had suffered for years from a serious respiratory illness and recently underwent a tracheotomy." Jump to new paragraph: "Deleuze was born in 1925 into a conservative Paris family."

Read between the lines.

*

If you could pray, would you ask for a sudden death rather than a long-winded, expected one? Or would you pray for forgiveness for what you are about to do?

Do not be sad when death arrives, someone somewhere might have said. Welcome and accept it rather than crying like a lost child.

Fleischmann couldn't help it.

Cats can't help it.

Some say there are worse things than death.

A man like Fleischmann may not ever think the way a philosopher thinks, but he'll immediately eat a banana or climb a tree without stopping to think.

If he could speak, maybe he would say: This constant buzzing in my head. Make it stop please. If you do, I'll stop. I'll stop slapping and scratching and crawling like an animal. At least animals dream.

The philosopher Gilles Deleuze threw himself out the window. Whether it was sudden or done with forethought, no one really knows. Maybe he did it because he suffered physically for several years. Maybe.

Someone somewhere said: "Think before you leap," and this saying eventually became a platitude, a cliché.

A philosopher normally starts from a position of thinking and ends in a position of thinking. Maybe.

Cats stare through the waking hours. Some say they dream. Daydream? Maybe. In between.

*

Addendum: What does one have to do with the other? Read carefully, and if you do, it will all come together.

WATCH OUT FOR
HIGHWAY WORKERS

A woman crossed the street in the early evening hours and a car struck her dead. It was reported that she had just left a house party in honor of Father's Day.

A young man hitched a ride in Mexico. The brakes on the truck failed, which led to the truck careening off a cliff. The accident resulted in seven fatalities, including the young man.

A man fell asleep at the wheel and lost control of his car. He swerved sideways across the freeway and another vehicle slammed into his at high speed. The other vehicle carried two—the driver and one passenger. No fatalities reported. The three involved complained of minor injuries.

The pedestrian's name was Sandra. She was 47 years old.

The hitchhiker is reported as the only American fatality. The others were of Mexican descent.

The man who fell asleep on the road stands at 6'2" with red hair. His name is Ken and his license plates are from Arizona.

The house party Sandra attended was not in honor of her father but for the father of her best friend Connie. Sandra's father died when she was three. She never knew her father but kept a sepia-colored photo of him on her refrigerator, pinned up with a rose-colored F-shaped magnet. She only went to the party for Connie's father because it happened to be Father's Day, which falls on a

Sunday every year. Sundays are Sandra's only day off. Every other day is devoted to various routine tasks.

The American hitchhiker, Rick, was on the dream trip of his lifetime. He was at the tail end of his tour of the Mexican state of Chihuahua. He died on a Sunday. It also happened to be the day before his 37th birthday.

The driver with the Arizona license plates never met the two women in the other vehicle. His name is Ken. Ken was informed that the names of the opposing claimants are Susanna and Amanda. Ken suffered a minor injury to his hand, which he insisted on caring for himself, while Susanna and Amanda suffered from chest and neck pains, which sent them to the ER. That same night they spent a total of six hours in the waiting room. They discovered that the reason for this long wait time was that there was another car collision that same day, reporting several fatalities.

Sandra used to collect anything and everything to do with roses, both real and manufactured. One Sunday morning at her favorite flower shop, she admired a bouquet of roses with her fingertips, raising one rose to her nostrils to enjoy its fragrance. She pricked herself on a thorn and winced as she licked the spot of blood from her pointer finger. She bought the whole bouquet, set it on top of the TV, and watched it more than the television show. The dozen roses were carefully arranged with three in front, three on each side and three in back. The primary rose—the one that pricked her—sat in the middle front row. The fragrance filled the room until the next morning when she dumped the bouquet into the trash.

There was no cab on the truck. The truck was new. No one knows for sure why the brakes failed. An ongoing investigation is expected to reveal the true cause of the accident. It is apparent that six of the eight passengers sat in the back of the truck. All six died of major injuries. It so happened that the only two survivors were the only children in the group, an infant and nine-year-old who had been sitting inside the truck where they were found with only minor injuries. The driver—who obviously was also inside the truck—died.

A single rose was found on the road where Sandra was hit. When asked, no one who attended the Father's Day party remembered whether Sandra took a rose from the two party bouquets with her.

Rick's car could not be found for weeks after his death. It was speculated that someone noticed his car sitting close to the border without movement and so took the opportunity to steal it. An investigation led to an arrest. The car had been stripped. Luckily there were no items of value left in it. Rick's backpack, with his valuables, was found further down the cliff, including a one-use camera with photos of his Mexico trip.

Amanda drove a two-year old Toyota Corolla that her father had given her as a gift. Her car was totaled in the accident. Amanda and Susanna remain best friends. Though they live countries apart (Susanna in Germany and Amanda in America), they post frequent status updates and current photos on Facebook that show no trace of the trauma incurred on that Easter Sunday. Amanda keeps photos in a private folder on her computer. She doesn't look at them, just as she doesn't look at the photos of her mother lying in a coffin.

Shortly after the accident, Susanna said, "Everything happens for a reason." Amanda's response was, "Hmmm."

Susanna made this statement while she and Amanda rode in the car driven by Amanda's father, who had been in a serious collision the year before. In fact, no less than four of Amanda's family members have been involved in a collision.

Rick had never been in a car accident of any kind before the one in which he died.

Sandra had never been struck by a car before.

Ken had never struck a car before.

Rick had been a volunteer many times. He had been a volunteer with Engineers Without Borders.

Amanda had never volunteered for anything except for the library book fair in her freshman year of college. This was part of a required Community Service Project and therefore does not count as real volunteer service.

Several of Rick's friends speculated that he must have offered up his body as a human shield for the two children who miraculously survived the accident. They were not yet aware of the fact that the two children sat inside of the vehicle while Rick sat in the back.

Amanda had met Rick two weeks after her accident at a friend's house party. She told him and two others about her accident. How the airbags deployed, causing her pains in the chest. How she felt traumatized. He said, while rubbing her arm, "At least you're alive." Amanda had only met Rick once because he died in that tragic truck accident in Mexico a month later. She had planned to meet him some more.

Shortly after the accident, Susanna told Amanda, "I was praying right after it happened." Amanda's response was, "Aha." Amanda had not prayed because she had not believed in God. She still doesn't.

Rick didn't have a chance to pray. This is what is assumed. He died instantly. His loved ones hope he died instantly so he wouldn't suffer.

Amanda and Susanna suffered because they lived.

Sandra might have suffered.

Amanda still doesn't know what really caused the accident. She has a hard time believing the police report, which quotes Ken as saying: "I fell asleep for a second."

The accident occurred shortly after 9 in the morning.

Amanda's car is the only one that collided with Ken's on a freeway containing other moving vehicles.

Everything happens for a reason.

You build it—It can fail.

An apple falls—not floats—from a tree.

$E = mc^2$.

It's like this see. Material, moving objects within the same atmosphere = encounters, collisions, explosions, implosions. According to Collision Theory, for a reaction to occur, molecules must collide. This is the theory. Man is the story.

Amanda does not express her spoken responses very well. She prefers the written word. "Just teaches you to enjoy the moment. Live. Really live, man." To which she writes: We live somewhere between memory and fantasy. Never here. Never now. It only appears that one has lived here and now, after he has left his trace.

She still doesn't know why she lived and why he died. She stopped asking why, taking the human out of the equation.

A 53-year old highway worker was struck dead this morning on the off-ramp of Highway 15. He will be replaced by a 32-year old worker first thing in the morning.

The first highway message board on Highway 15 reads: Safety Alert! WATCH OUT FOR HIGHWAY WORKERS.

Another message board half a mile down the highway reads: WATCH OUT FOR HIGHWAY WORKERS.

Watch out.

NOT THIS TOWN

The fact that it happened at the town's polar bear research station is irrelevant. A polar bear didn't kill the child. The day shift station janitor just happened to have his pet bear with him that day. He happened to own a bear that he kept as a pet in his basement. One day – the day of the tragedy – Janitor Man's basement flooded and so he had no choice but to take Bear with him to work. Bear remained in the cage in the back of Janitor Man's van while he worked his shift.

But this story isn't really about Janitor Man or Bear, not even about the child who was killed. Child—the victim of the tragedy let's call it—cannot be adequately described because he died before the age of five, before the age of a stable, unique identity. In what psychoanalysts call the imaginary, he was not able to separate himself from Bear or any other object in the world. So, we can assume that in a sense, when Bear consumed him, Child was already part of Bear and Bear part of Child.

Are you following? Think about it. It isn't lazy to refrain from offering a detailed description of a toddler who wobbles like all other toddlers and excuse the nomenclature—"they all look the same," eyes too big for their heads, drooling mouths more gums and lips than teeth. Already I go too far.

This story isn't even about the polar bear research station that made the town famous by its advanced research capabilities, or how a simpleton like Janitor Man ended up working there. As hard as it may be to accept as coincidence, the fact that the station researches bears, and that Janitor Man owned a bear really is coincidental. One might imagine that what drew him to the station in the first place is the residence of specimen bears, considering that he chose a bear as a pet; he must be drawn to all bears. Such reasoning would be like assuming that because I have children of my own, I will choose a place of work involving children in the workplace, like a hospital or school, which isn't so. In fact, say I so dislike my job of raising children (I have two of my own), I have chosen (whether subconsciously or unconsciously) a career that for the most part, avoids the presence of any children at all. Say I work in a cubicle set off by twelve other cubicles by foldable walls for the state historical society, as say an assistant editor. My coworkers and I are not allowed to bring their children to work.

This is pure conjecture. I am the all-knowing narrator and thus do not own a stable, identifiable identity.

This story isn't about me either. This mini narrative is about assumptions, as you might have guessed. The town with the renowned polar bear research station assumed the child was merely missing, rather than consumed. I know what you're thinking. The two are not mutually exclusive. That is, when one, like Child, is said to have been consumed, eaten and digested, one could also be said to be missing, in that one is simply not there anymore. Forgive me if my words form as grotesque a mental picture in your head as it does in mine, assuming of course that you're imagining Bear tearing in to poor Child's body—head first maybe, then neck and limbs, or another stage in the process, the end of it all where only bits and parts remain, kind of like road kill, only Child wasn't killed on the road. He was killed in the back of Janitor Man's van. Let me explain.

For this story to be complete, we need to return to the acquisition of Bear by Janitor Man. If this story has all the expected fixings. I the all-knowing.

You'll say the notion of a man—or anyone for that matter—owning a pet bear and keeping it in the basement is a stretch of the imagination. If you've wandered around this world enough, you'll know that stranger things have happened.

You're sitting at the hair salon inside Wal-Mart, waiting to get 15 foils of blond highlights for the special price of $39.99. A fella who looks like he might be named Bubba strides in wearing a dirty football jersey and looking for LuLu. He asks D.J., the gal who's appointed to do your hair, "Where's LuLu?" Bubba need a haircut bad. He's playing semi-pros tonight and he's gotta look good. D.J. says LuLu isn't working a shift today on account of being sick. *"Shee-it!"* says Bubba, who come to find is named Travis after all. "Me and LuLu go way back," Travis adds, "hell we used to date. I need her to get her ass in here asap!" D.J. in her soft-spoken way says, "Well if you wait just a minute while I get this client going, I'll go on and give you her number," and you think to yourself, can one not quote a phone number while mixing hair paint? "We go way back too," Travis repeats, "we've known each other since we were 16. Well alright then," Travis says as he plops his big ass in that there chair, staring at you with five foils now attached to your hair. You allow your eyes to dwell on the page in your book longer than it takes to read a page of that length. You can feel Travis staring while he twirls around in the chair, kicking up his cowboy-booted feet. D.J. finally quotes LuLu's number, which makes you cringe, not because you care one way or another, but because D.J. ought not to have given her "we-go-way- back" friend's number away so easily, to the first stranger claiming loyal friendship, the first Bubba or Travis to come storming in. Travis makes a show of it—dialing LuLu's number 949-822-1343. You repeat the number in your head rather than reading the same page you've been on for ten minutes. You wait to hear Travis curse because maybe he's reached Pizza Hut instead, but apparently Lu-Lu has answered the phone and will be there in ten. Wow. So Travis brags, we go way back, she's my gal. She'll be here. Meanwhile, Travis repeats the fact that he plays semi-pro football in Arlington, Texas. "Why do you have to say Texas, I know Arlington is in Texas," D.J. smart-assedly says. "Well", says Travis, in his mock smart voice, "you know there is an Arlington, Virginia." "Really?" D.J. says, and you're kind of amazed that there's a shade of intelligence in that looks-like-a-peach head. "I have a game tonight," he says, "either that or me and my buds will go gambling." Way to go Trav. The semi-pros mean so much to you. The stains on his shirt say he's already played. Or maybe he stuck his hand in his behind and wiped it on said shirt. The way his jeans sag down and show his big-ass butt crack tells you that he might have pulled an all-nighter. Travis is loud, and he's scary. He's only waited for like two minutes and he dials LuLu again, "Get your ass over here girl, asap!" "Hey," D.J. says with a slightly raised voice, "hold your horses. If you really know LuLu like I do, you know she will whip your ass for talking like that." "Yeah right," Travis drawls, and you can't believe you're getting your hair cut inside a Wal-Mart, with a guy who should be named Bubba staring at your hair, in flesh and blood, like a scene out of trailer-trash TV, too stereotypical or ridiculous to be reality. You're taking mental notes.

In comes LuLu in sweatpants and wet hair. "I thought you was sick," says Bubba/ Travis. This won't be pretty. "Hell Lu, what took you so damn long?" Lu hits Travis upside the head and pinches his ear and tells him not to curse or swear. This is a fine family establishment. D.J. puts you under the dryer and gives you the eye, the one that says these people have issues, and then she says, "These people have issues."

In and out of consciousness of the place where you are, you learn that this town you live in really is small. You've been living here for only three months, and already you know that LuLu and Travis used to be a thing, that LuLu is now single two boyfriends later, the last one having shouted something on a street corner when LuLu ran after him, something like: "Later, Bitch!" You put two and two together and surmise that Travis and LuLu are probably not presently sleeping together, and that LuLu puts up with a lot of crap. You reason that D.J. and LuLu are likely better friends. D.J. stays at this lousy minimum wage paying job for LuLu's sake, who does not want to work here without her best friend. Something about Travis, who says he went and kicked the ass of some fella to a pulp. You don't know for what. You assume it didn't take much to light Travis' fuse. Something about some chick being a bitch because she smokes and drinks while being pregnant, even stalking men, at bars, bitch shouldn't be at bars. "Well that ain't no thing," interjects LuLu, after all this is small town Texas. Still, Travis hates that bitch. It occurs to you that one day you will probably run into Lulu, or D.J., or Bubba/Travis by pure coincidence in the town square. And you do. You recognize the bad haircut and jersey, which is now clean.

Stranger things have happened perhaps, yes. The latter story might meet the standard of a little less strange than stranger things, which means we're talking about a range, the range of strange things. Janitor Man did not get his pet bear from a circus, which you might assume. He went camping one summer with a couple of buddies when they were attacked by hungry bears. I all-knowing, there was only one bear, and it was a cub that came upon their camp with great hunger. Bear knocked down their sardine and beer cans, which made a ruckus in the dead of night, which woke them from their tents and sleeping bags. Janitor Man's buddies were not about to go and help him take the cub home, knowing it was illegal and all. I all-knowing, am not lazy. This part of the narrative counts as irrelevant. Let's just jump to the part where Janitor Man felt quite taken with Bear, whom he fed the last can of Black and Tan. They became instant friends, as Bear was yet Baby Bear and not of the age to make a killing, of a large human being. Janitor Man named little bear, Bubba. That's how the latter story is relevant. For now on we'll call Bear Bubba.

Admit it. You want to jump to the part about Bubba tearing into Child, who still has no identifiable name. This story isn't about Child; it's about the town and its assumptions. But since I cannot narrate the story of the assuming town without touching on what it is they assumed upon, I will tell you the parts of the Bubba/Child story that will elucidate them and their assumptions.

The day was glorious, in the way the sun—once it came

up—stayed so sunny in the sky, shining on all those in the town. The breeze coming through the just-enough-of-a-crack in the back of the van windows stirred Bubba in the way only a Bear can be stirred. Bubba happened to also be hungry. As you might have guessed, Child was left unattended by his single-parent mommy who (against the station's rules) brought Child to work in lieu of leaving him at home, as babysitter called in sick with the stomach flu. How did Child get into the van? I all-knowing, happen not to know that part of the story. However, it's safe to assume that Janitor Man unwittingly left the door unlocked—no—part way open, as Child was too small to understand that the door of the van was unlocked. But hanging partway open—

Say Child managed to get into the back of the van, and say inadvertently unlatched the door to the cage, which Janitor Man, in his hurriedness that morning left unlocked. Now Bubba is a bear, not a man, and as such must feed his hunger indiscriminately. Maybe Child would have survived if he had pooped his pants, because this species of a bear is not known to eat humans who smell of human excrement. But as Child was past the diaper stage and fully potty-trained, he smelled just like bacon and eggs, which is what his neglectful mother fed him that morning. The rest, well, I'll leave to your imagination.

Back to the town and its assumptions. Bubba in fact, ate all of Child, leaving not a trace, except for the nipple part of his pacifier. You'll say that earlier I led you to believe that bits of Child remained. Let me remind you that that was what I had imagined, and as you're aware, we as human beings have the faculty of initiating mental images without any prior facticity. That's what I did, and what I assume you did, imagine the worst-case scenario. Which isn't to say that being completely devoured is worse or better than the other possibility.

Once Child was nowhere to be found, and the allotted time of 24 hours had passed, Child's mother and her kin and friends assumed that Child was only missing. That Child was mysteriously missing, from their sight, vicinity, from their very lives. They didn't jump to the latter assumption until much later, something like a year and two weeks.

They and the town assumed the usual suspects—kidnapping, or wandering into the woods, where he'd eventually be found. Maybe the reason the town did not assume the truth, that in fact Child was eaten by Bubba the Bear, is because no one knew that Janitor Man owned a pet bear, which he took to work that tragic day. Even his buddies who watched him capture Bubba as a cub didn't know that Janitor Man made the tragic decision to have Bubba accompany him to the Polar Bear Research station, the only place where bears can legally dwell other than the state zoo. If only Janitor Man had asked his bosses permission to keep Bubba in a cage in one of the observatory rooms, perhaps Child would be here today, all grown into a fully formed human being with an identifiable name, part of the symbolic order, where bears sometimes represent man's kinship to the animal kingdom so well, depending on the context. This brings us to Janitor Man and his knowing. Relevant or not, you decide, he was the only one who knew that Bubba killed Child. He did not assume; he knew with the lucidity of someone in possession of all his faculties. The remaining pacifier gave it away, yes. But even if the thought crossed his mind that this was mere coincidence, he knew—as well as he knew the workings of a hungry bear, which is why he kept the horrid secret to himself. Why should Bubba pay the price for acting by pure instinct? Janitor Man knew that confessing on the part of Bubba would not bring poor Child back.

Even if the town found out that Janitor Man owned a pet bear, we can assume that the idea of Bubba the adorable brown bear consuming a four-year-old child inside a van on the polar bear research station premises, with no witnesses to speak of, would never cross their minds. All they do in this town is un-reflect. They mingle among one another passively in a state of banality, thinking upon matters not too terribly strange. So that even if the thought of a bear tearing into the body of a small child did in fact cross their minds, it would not remain and blossom there. Not there. Maybe it would in another world much stranger than theirs.

NOT HERE

(Indirectly inspired by the Tarkovsky film, Stalker*)*

The Changer stands in front of three padlocks, which hang on a chain chained to a chain-linked fence. A red and white sign hangs directly above the padlocks: "NO LOITERING NEXT TO FENCE." Beyond the fence is a man-made reservoir.

Disregarding the NO LOITERING sign, the Changer stands close to the fence for thirty minutes. He then turns to his friend the Oral Writer, who is standing a few feet behind him. "What do I smell like?" he asks. The Oral Writer takes a whiff of the Changer and says, "You smell like rust and pine." Glaring up at the sign, the Changer then slips his wrists into the chains that chain the chain-link fence.

The Oral Writer, who only speaks aloud what he has already written, has never written anything addressing a gesture of this kind; therefore, he has nothing to say. The Not-Here is over there, some distance on the other side of the fence. He observes the Changer struggling within the confines of the chains. He ponders over whether his friendship with the Changer is of any use in this situation, given the fact that the Changer stakes little value in the value of friendship. The Not-Here decides not to interfere.

In the Changer's experience, friendship is as burdensome as the chains that now chain him to the chain-link fence. The more friends he accumulates, the more projections he must suffer. Take this immediate situation: to his friend the Oral Writer, he smells like rust and pine, probably because he loiters next to the padlocks, which smell of rust and pine; however, he wishes that for once, he could smell as nature has granted rather than circumstance.

The Changer wriggles in his self-imposed chains. The Oral Writer senses frustration in this most symbolic representation and so explores his toolbox of sayings and phrasings that would address the Changer's plight. He does not have the ability (nor the sense) to discern the difference between the objectivity of an object and the subjectivity of his friend. His ability is with words; he can tame the words that form in his brain by writing them down and arranging them in interesting variations. At last, he finds a saying that possibly relates to the Changer's dilemma; therefore, he speaks it aloud: "Man imitates nature, then sets up prohibitions that mirror his own fears and judgments; whereas, nature welcomes man to roam, explore and discover its challenges for themselves." A stretch? Perhaps. But in this unique formulation, the Oral Writer senses a possible escape for his friend.

The Changer ruminates upon his friend's pronouncement aloud, "This lake is manmade, and so a mock form of nature. But it's been here so long so that it is now populated with geese, ducks, swans and so on. It functions just like a real lake. Is it artificial or now a part of nature?"

"I think you already know the answer to your own question," the Oral Writer says. Instantly he slaps his hand to his mouth. He recognizes this arrangement of words as a platitude, spoken an infinite number of times by others before him.

The Changer loses concentration on this exchange of words and continues to wriggle in frustration. Why? To the other (in this case his friend the Oral Writer) he smells like the objects he is in the vicinity of (or is it *like the objects that are in his vicinity?*) Not only does he smell like rust and pine to his friend the Oral Writer, he now begins to smell like the padlocks to himself. He even feels like he is the objects that he smells like—hard and cold and unrelenting. As he begins losing any sense of himself, he can hardly bear it and so casts a pleading look at the Not-Here. The Not-Here cannot act in behalf of his friends until they make a first move, and he recognizes this look of distress as an emergency call for his friendship. The Changer maintains a focus on his distant friend the Not-Here, and he immediately removes his wrists from the chains, releasing himself. The chains chaining the chain-linked fence fall to the ground.

"What is impossible for one becomes mastery with two." Although the Changer has grown weary with these platitudes, he nonetheless senses that the Oral Writer is right. "You already know the answer to your own question." The manmade lake is now a part of nature, and if he is ever to be released from enslavement to the projections of others, he must trespass into the place founded by others.

The Oral Writer and the Changer arrive at the foot of the lake. Somewhere over there, not by the foot of the lake is the Not-Here. The first creatures the three friends see are three geese.

"Can you sleep standing on one leg? Neck craned backwards, head resting on a soft white feather bed. You are not a goose. You are only a man."

"So, you are a poet too?" says the Changer. The Oral Writer nods his head, admiring these white geese that look the same as the ones he has seen at the edge of a lake not made by man.

"Man is not much of anything. Why, then, must I conform to his projections? Man's sign says: NO LOITERING. I am judged as a loiterer merely by standing next to a fence. I stand next to a fence that smells like rust and pine, and I am judged as smelling of rust and pine."

The Oral Writer recognizes the overall meaning of these words as very similar to something he's written before. However, he decides not to quote it aloud, not only to avoid redundancy but to avoid revealing—to the Changer's dismay—that it's not only his smell that suffers the projections of others but every other aspect of himself as well (such as standing next to a fence makes him a loiterer.)

"Disregard the sign, therefore smell like rust and pine." The Changer cannot tell if these words have come from the Not-Here or the Oral Writer. The Not-Here has hardly ever spoken aloud, but when he has, it is fleeting and profound. He is never here, but over there, because he infinitely thrusts himself into the future; the here and now is constantly being made past for the beyond. And now, already, the Changer is beginning to smell like something else.

Before anyone can sense what it is, the geese fluster awake. The three friends are careful not to get too close to the beaks of the geese. The geese waddle into the manmade lake. When they are far enough from the shore, the Oral Writer and Changer move closer to the shimmering water. The Changer looks down at his reflection. It ripples. A small stone skips on the water. And then another. When he looks up, he sees it is his friend the Oral Writer who is skipping stones. "Look again. This is you, but within nature's boundaries." The Changer observes the contours of his face wave and bounce. He is fascinated at the notion that man and nature have joined to create this reflection of his face. He is not troubled but rather intrigued. He looks up at the geese, in the middle of the lake now, gliding on the waters and unaware (or without care) that they are imprisoned within this manmade reservoir. They do not seem to suffer from man's mocking of nature, nor their displacement from their original home. They reside within a compromise.

The Changer turns to the Oral Writer. "You said that I smelled like rust and pine. This is what you sensed. Your sense became my sense, so that my sense was lost. You believe you have no control over your senses. But maybe you do. Already I am beginning to smell like something else, but strangely, I do not know of what yet. That must mean you are not sure either." The Changer draws closer to his friend. "Smell me now, and before you analyze the surroundings, tell me what I really smell like."

"Why, that is simply absurd." This is the Oral Writer's stock answer to the propounding of most human ideas, and often, it works in discouraging even the most ingenious of minds. The Changer is not ingenious, but he is insistent.

"Go on, smell me." The Oral Writer sniffs the Changer's neck. "Before you tell me what I smell like, I can tell you that I once smelled like sweet ginger snap. That is the smell of my birth."

The Oral Writer scratches his head. Before he answers, he scribbles something in his notebook, considering that the circumstances call for an arrangement of words never required before.

"You still smell of pine and rust." The Changer shuts his eyes, taking a whiff of himself.

"Already you've made a small compromise."

"How so?"

"You mentioned pine before rust, whereas previously it was rust and pine." The tensed muscles in the Changer's face begin to relax, and he forms what appears to be a grin.

Already the Not-Here is on the other side of the lake past a "No Swimming" sign visible amidst heavy brush. His two friends pick up on his trail, and considering he is always one step ahead of them, he is submerged in the water up to his chin when they arrive. The Changer recognizes a swim in the lake as an opportunity to wash away his current smell of pine and rust. True, he no longer smells of rust and pine (the scent of pine now outweighs the rust); however, he prefers no smell at all to the smell imposed by others. Certainly, to wash away the smell will be a challenge, as he has no soap on hand. Not that soap would do any good. His previous experiences with soap and water have always left him frustrated, as even the most generic of soaps invites the faintest of impressions. Once he soaped himself with an advertised "non-scented soap," yet his wife told him he smelled like lavender. The smell of lavender gives him headaches, and so he scrubbed himself with lye. She then said he smelled like cleanliness itself, which was too sterile for her taste.

Apparently, neither the Not-Here, the Changer, nor the Oral Writer have asked themselves why the manmade sign forbids swimming in the lake. Given that it's natural to swim in a lake, they don't hesitate—except for the Changer.

The Changer is not a very good swimmer, and so at

first, he hesitates. However, he assumes that still water is safer than a moving stream or the waves of the ocean. As he doggie paddles into deeper water, he loses his momentum and starts sinking. The Oral Writer grabs him by the arm and guides him to the surface, not saying a word.

As they swim to shore, the Changer searches for the Not-Here, ahead of them where he ought to be. He is nowhere to be seen. For these few moments, he has forgotten himself. But when they reach land, the Changer will once again be concerned with what he smells like, seeking to return to the smell of his birth. He is not aware that the smell of sweet ginger snaps at birth was the smell projected by his mother and was thus not granted by nature. Nature grants nothing but the playground in which to perceive an array of sights, sounds, tastes and smells. Perhaps ginger snaps were placed on a plate by the hospital bed. Unable to withstand the smell of birth, which for her was the smell of pain, she immediately transferred the pleasant smell of ginger snaps to her newborn son. The more likely story is that he was born smelling like nothing, and his mother simply could not bear this smell of nothing. Therefore, the Changer will always smell like something, even when this something is nothing.

The Changer is still not certain. Sometimes he picks up a faint scent of his very own, even among the objects of his world. When he withdrew from this manmade lake, he smelled something like a cross between soggy cookies and a Christmas tree. But the Oral Writer, the Changer, and the Not-Here are not here anymore. Neither are the three geese. They are—each one of them—over there somewhere.

RED BALLOON

Oh, look at the moon. All shining up there.
Oh, how she looks like a lamp in the air.

Today, I return to the distant past. I close my eyes and try to possess my childhood self. At first, she resists, but then opens her (my) eyes to the pages of memory: a blond little boy in blue overalls, followed by a floating red balloon. She wants that balloon, and so do I.

I'm holding Mama's hand. I beg her to buy me that bag of balloons, the mixed-assortment kind. The bag has balloons of many colors—white, yellow, blue. But a single red balloon flashes brightest of them all. I squeeze the crinkling plastic bag where the red balloon resides. I want this red balloon and suddenly it is mine.

Before I blow it up, I write a little message on a small piece of paper and insert it inside. I grasp a spool of white thread from Mama's sewing basket and unravel just enough to tie to the balloon and let it bounce up and down. Tying the string onto the balloon, I hold on tight like the boy in the overalls. If I don't, it (or I) might fly away.

I wander around the streets of my neighborhood. Window shutters and iron bars hovering, towers with needle tops pointing towards the sky. *You wish you were Pascal, the little French boy, don't you?* she says to me, my childhood self. Am I remembering it as it really was or as I had wished it to be?

There are simple neighborhood houses, one or two stories high, with large yards and wire fences separating one house from the other, each one with a face of its own. I am 6 or 7 years old. I tie the red balloon to my wrist now so it will stay with me wherever I go. I feel as if I am drifting, floating by these homes, half me and half my childhood self.

Suddenly water sprays my face. The water spews from a snakelike hose. The hose is pinned down into the ground of a green-carpeted yard. A diapered baby splashes water in a round, portable pool. As I move along, I smell the Oscar Meyer hot dogs and 100-percent beef patties smoldering from a barbeque grill.

Dark-chocolate colored girls with corkscrew curls dig up dirt from their backyard, grime and sparkly mud all over their fingers and hands as they pat the mud into mud pies. Patty and Vanesha, the Guamanian sisters who lived next door. Patty the same age as me, Vanesha a little younger, with their yellow teeth and soiled white dresses. I join them in playing patty cake until sunset, before Mama and Papa call me back inside for supper.

A time when being a kid was all about games – marbles and Legos, Flatsy-Patsies and musical wind up merry-go-rounds. About playing outside just a little after dark. All this before my childhood things turned used and worn, sold in a garage sale, or piled away in a corner.

I see Vanesha's dirty white panties as she crouches. She's rolling up potato bugs and flicking them down the gutter. I take charge of the bugs, slicing a black ticker bug in half, watching the separated halves wiggle around. I remember walking home from school with the sisters, stopping by the Mendoza's a few houses away from mine, buying Mexican candy in their kitchen—Tamarindo pops for a quarter, tape candy for a nickel, and packs of saladitos for ten cents each. I'd pop open my green fish wallet by squeezing the head and tail together, dropping the coins onto Mrs. Mendoza's sweaty palm. Even before we left their porch, I would unwrap the tape candy slowly with my teeth and the sugary and sour taste would make my taste buds go wild. Vanesha would tap my arm with her sticky finger and offer me one of her Saladitos. Whatever happened to Patty and Vanesha? They must have moved away, back to their original home in Guam. I try to hold on, but they fade from view.

It will be dark soon, so I must find the best place for take-off.

I am at the beach, digging my toes into the wet sand, the red balloon bouncing in the air as I flap my arms up and down as if I were a bird. I flap them slowly, then wave them in half-circles rapidly until my arms become whirligigs. I'm nearly taken up and away! I open my eyes and find little ripples splashing against my ankles. I squint at a bright spot in the ocean, a shiny glare. Two bodies bounce in the waves, two silhouettes. I don't know how to swim, so I resist the urge to jump in and keep digging my toes into the dirt with my red balloon tied to my wrist. I want those strangers to stay out there, far away, whoever they are. They will ask me what I'm doing with this silly red balloon bobbing next to me like an extra head. They might laugh, or they might envy me and my beautiful, bright, perfectly shaped red balloon.

Maybe this is where I let my prized possession free, above the shallow waters, water up to my ankles, as I watch my red balloon rise. My heart sinks as my little friend becomes smaller and smaller and blends into the sun and sky.

But wait! she says, my childhood self. *This isn't where it happens.* I feel the grainy, warm sand in between my toes. True, I don't like it, never have. I don't like getting sand on my feet. Never have.

I try to remember the last time Mama and Papa took me to the beach, but I can't. What I remember is being scolded for dirtying the carpet with my shoes, Papa slamming his office door behind him and Mama dropping onto the couch, setting her feet on the coffee table and turning on the television. Her shoulders bent forward like an old coat hanger, asking me to come over and pluck the two white hairs from her scalp. I do, and she smiles with sad eyes.

She's right, my childhood self. This isn't where it happened.

It's nearly pitch dark, but for the light of the moon. There's just enough moonlight to see my feet as I step on the crisp, dry grass, and onto the little bank by the next-door neighbor's chain link fence. The next-door neighbor is an obese lady who constantly screams. One day I witnessed her pour water over her elderly mother as I peeked through the blinds in my bedroom. She lifted a tin pail over the white-haired head and the old lady jolted, shaking herself like a wet dog. Till this day I don't know if what she did was cruel (was the water piping hot? Or was this a case of a daughter washing her mother's hair by hand?)

My dog Odie is barking, pulling at his chain tied to the tool shed. I shush him but he keeps barking, wagging his golden tail. It sparkles, even in the darkness. I scoot myself further up the hill and hold the balloon string tight. I'm nearly ready, but first I will eat my midnight snack and drink from my green canteen. I'm on a little night adventure, my ding-dong wrapped in aluminum foil, and my canteen wrapped around my neck. I tie the balloon back onto my wrist and unwrap the foil as quietly as I can. It crinkles, and Odie stops barking, starts panting and begging. I bite into the hard chocolate crust, into the moist white cream. I wash it down with a little bottle of Sunny Delight. I wish there was someone to share this with. But no, just me, Odie, and the moonlight. As I untie the string one last time, my heart drops. My red balloon will travel further than I ever have or ever will. These are the words I printed in silvery ink: "Hello stranger. I have traveled far and seen many places and things. I don't know who you are, but it doesn't much matter because I've found you. This was meant to be. Please read, then do whatever you wish with this little note. Even though I don't know you, I love you."

My childhood self says nothing now. Maybe she is pleased. This is it. I can feel it, from my head, down to my toes.

I close my eyes and make a wish, a wish to the moon: Let your light be the guide. Then I let go. When I open my eyes, they are moist and sticky. I watch my friend float away into the smiling face in the sky.

MONKEY SQUARE

When I visit home, I don't recall anything of the past. Maybe that's because Dad is still there. Dad is there and alive. He and the house are now. He opens the door, and I don't notice he has only a few strands of hair left on his balding head, or that his chin is scrunched in more than before or that he's lost a few more teeth. If he were gone, then the dark paneled walls of the living room, the hippie-style beads still hanging from the kitchen doorway, and the sliding closet door loosened from its hinges would invite my memory right there and then to revisit the delights of childhood energy, bursting and anxious.

It's when I'm away from home and the neighborhood of my childhood that I remember things—insignificant and far removed from my adult life. An image, or the image of an object—that's all it takes to spark a memory. A balloon bobbing up and down in the hands of a child, a shiny new penny on the street. A sidewalk like any other.

A round piece of metal in the sidewalk in my new neighborhood. Taking a walk to the grocery store up the street, I saw it, just like the ones I discovered on Chestnut Avenue, where I grew up.

Monkey Square.

I spotted the first one on my walk home from school one day in fourth grade. It looked like a rusted penny from a distance, but when I bent down to pick it up it wouldn't budge; it was lodged in the ground, drilled into the sidewalk—a metal disk in the middle of the cement square. When I realized I couldn't lift it from the sidewalk, I moved on. Then a few feet further, I saw another one. This time the disk wasn't in the middle, but near the crack dividing this square from the next. I had spotted several randomly by the time I arrived home.

That night as I drifted into sleep I dreamed of circles and squares, dancing around one another, different colors and sizes. First, they danced, and then they merged, invading one another's space. I woke up in the middle of the night all drenched in sweat.

In fourth grade I walked to and from school alone. My mind was always active and alive, but hardly ever in the moment. I would live in the book I was reading at the time: Hazel Rah of *Watership Down,* his ghost floating away to join the Black Rabbit of Inle. My eyes stinging as I conjure up their shapes in front of me, black and white, gliding and swerving in the air until they disappear into the bushes or the trees. Anne, *Anne of Green Gables*—Carrots! I run after her and her freckles, carrot-colored hair, milk white skin, and tilt up of the chin. I want both Anne and to be Anne.

It took the little metal disks to bring me back into myself and to place my feet back on the ground.

After my first discovery I searched for more. I even went so far as to walk past my house to see if there were more up the street. There were. And I created a game with specific rules: When you spot the little round disk in a cement square, you can't step in it. You jump over the square. If you step in the square or don't jump far enough, you lose. Of course, the best part was spotting the monkey square in time to make the leap. These were the rules I created, and that was the name I gave it: Monkey Square.

At first, I didn't mind playing my game alone, but then it became dull. There was no one to cheer me on when I made it over the square, and no one to make fun of should they step inside one by mistake. I had no one to walk home from school with, so I continued playing by myself, to quiet my noisy mind.

I could have invited Scottie, a boy in my fourth-grade class, to play with me, but he was gross. I caught him a few times in the neighborhood kneeling on the dirty curb, licking at the water running down the cracks in the sidewalk—water from people watering their lawns or washing their cars. He used to suck on my hair in third grade while we watched Disney movies. The first time it happened, I felt my head pull back, and when I turned around, I saw him sucking on my long hair like it was a licorice stick. I was about to tell him to stop, but then he pulled it out of his mouth, smiled wide with his two front teeth missing and didn't seem at all embarrassed or surprised.

I couldn't ask him to play with me after he asked me to go around. He was walking on the opposite side of the street, but I felt him staring.

"Hey Abigail!"

"It's Abby," I said, glaring over at him. No one called me Abigail except for Mom and Dad. He remained on the other side of the street for a time, but then without my invitation crossed over to my side. I'd been playing Monkey Square on my own as usual, and he interrupted my game. "Hey Abby," he said much softer now, "Wanna go around?" He reached his hand towards me and instantly I tucked my chin in turtle-like. I thought he was going to touch my neck. I had a phobia that left me fearful of necklaces and turtlenecks. My cheeks felt hot, as they did whenever I was the center of attention, but this time I was blazing from my neck up into my eyelids. No one had ever asked me to go around. Most of the boys called me toothpick, Olive Oil, or beanpole, including Scottie. I looked at his dirty blond shaggy hair covering his eyes and didn't know what to say. He kept walking with me, and I was afraid he could see the safety pin keeping my khaki colored pants from falling off my waist, or the masking tape keeping the hems of my pants from dragging on the ground.

"Well?" he asked.

"I don't think so," I answered without looking up. Scottie said nothing as he walked back across the street, the cuffs of his jeans making a swooshing sound as he walked faster.

When he turned the corner, I searched for the next Monkey Square, but instead I found a dark rectangular hole in the sidewalk where the slab was missing. As I leaped over the hole, I feared landing in an endless tunnel, pulling me down, down, down into my dreams—the one of Barbies without their clothes on, on top of shiny new cars. Naked, not naked dolls but naked women – women with curvy bodies. Barbies. Barbie games. Making them kiss, Ken on top of Barbie, mashing their naked bodies against each other—my face and neck heating up. Barbie on top of Ken, but can't make the kissing sounds.

I played Monkey Square regularly and alone until I became distracted with Richard. I discovered Richard the summer right before fifth grade. I don't know how this happened, but it did:

As I prepared to scrub the bathroom down, I stepped onto the bathtub to slide the window open. That's when I spotted Cinda, my next-door neighbor, swinging in her backyard, talking to herself. I watched her for a few moments, then yelled out, "Hi Cinda, this is Rrrrrrrichard!" in a high, falsetto voice.

I became Richard beginning at noon when Mom started her daily, hours-long ritual of watching her favorite soap operas, *General Hospital* and *Days of Our Lives*. Cinda would be swinging on her homemade device of plywood and jump ropes, talking to herself. Our backyard was large with two trees, a clothesline and a tool shed, but the wall with the bathroom window was just a few yards away from chain link fence, which separated her yard from mine. I'd step onto the bathtub, slide open the window and start talking to her with my Richard voice. She'd dart her head up quick like a startled cat but couldn't see through the frosted glass window that I slid open just enough for her to hear me, but not see me. I'd repeat, "Hi Cinda, this is Richard." Then she'd ask, "Who's that?" I'd say, "I'm Richard your friend." Her eyes would dart back and forth, up and down, while she slowed her swinging to a halt. "Where are you? Why don't you come out and play?"

Coming out to play with Cinda was not an option. Not only was she my next-door neighbor, we went to the same school. She was an E.D. kid, emotionally disturbed. On the playground, she would turn red, start to shake and snap her teeth like a mad dog, and I never knew why. Her special class could play with the *normal* kids under the supervision of Ms. Rickenbacker. Ms. Rickenbacker was skinnier than I was, hip bones showing through her polyester pants, her face sunken in like a skull. Sometimes Cinda would ask Ms. Rickenbacker if she could play dodge ball and she'd let her, but only if she promised not to play too rough. One time she pelted a fifth-grade boy so hard in the face with the red rubber ball that he started to cry. Cinda then turned and gave him one of her great big bear hugs and wouldn't let go. When Ms. Rickenbacker's male helper managed to pry her away, he had to restrain her from behind as she started kicking her feet against the hot afternoon wind.

Cinda was a stocky kid with long blond hair almost white in the sun. She was neither pretty nor ugly. But her twisted, red face seemed scary when she had her fits. I wondered what made Cinda the way she was. I thought maybe something bad happened to her, and she needed to let all that rage out somehow.

Maybe she felt like I did when Mom and Dad screamed at each other so loud that it shook the house. I'd scream into my pillow till I nearly suffocated. During one of their worse screaming episodes, I took a pair of scissors and chopped off my hair until I was left with short, uneven bangs. It felt good doing this as I watched the long pieces of black hair fall all over my lap.

I loved our secret game—Cinda's and mine. And it continued into fifth grade.

It always started off the same way, whether right after school or on the weekend. I'd talk in my high voice and then ask her what she was doing and was she being a good little girl. Cinda told Richard that she didn't like playing alone, and how most of the kids at school didn't like her. I told her I would always be her friend. Richard, not Abby. At school, I secretly wanted to play with her because she was good at wall-ball and kicking the soccer ball real far. But if I did, I wouldn't hear the end of it from the other kids. I wanted her to teach me how to kick the ball, as I always seemed to miss or at best, kick only a few feet in front of me.

My mind and heart were restless, and I realized that if I played with Cinda in my backyard or hers, there would be no one there to see. Still, I couldn't bring myself to knock on her door and ask if she could come out and play. Mom wouldn't have let me anyway. She called Cinda's mom that "white, wild woman," raising her crazy daughter without a husband. But it didn't matter to me what Mom said. I liked how pale Cinda's face and hair looked in the sunshine, as if they were one and the same, compared to my black hair and brown skin. I liked our game the way it was, and I enjoyed being Richard.

One day my Richard game took a turn.

"Come closer," I said to Cinda. I mean Richard said. She came off the swing and stepped closer to the fence, following the sound of the voice but still not finding it. Then after a few moments' hesitation, she clung to the fence and stuck her lips between the wires. They were cherry-colored, sparkling like the wet-kiss lip-gloss Mom had bought me for my last birthday. As I stood on the bathtub, my legs began to tire, shaking at the knees.

"Where are you?" she said louder than usual, darting her eyes again. "Remember our rules?" I said. "You can never see me, but I'll call your name often and talk to you often." I peeked through the window, trying to keep my head low, even though I knew she couldn't see me through the frosted glass. Just then, her mother slid their backdoor open.

"Cinda, what's going on?" She rushed towards Cinda and unglued her from the fence. She looked suspiciously up towards the window as I crouched down, holding onto the edge of the windowpane. I nearly slipped into the bathtub when I heard rustling of dry grass and the patio door slam shut. I held my breath and snuck back into my bedroom, shutting my door ever so quietly. I was terrified that the doorbell would ring, and that Cinda's mom would uncover my secret game. I knew what had to be done. I would have to tuck Richard away, somewhere back where he came from.

The next day, I snuck up to the window to see if Cinda was playing in her backyard, and there she was, on the swing. "Richard, are you there?" she said in a strained voice, trying to keep me a secret. When I didn't answer, she said a little louder, "Richard, where are you? I miss you." I wanted so badly to answer, but I was scared her mom was waiting inside, peeking out and listening to see if Richard would answer, so I didn't. Poor Cinda, she looked so sad.

The following week at morning recess Cinda was playing on the swings. I saw her as I hung by my legs from the monkey bars. My long hair hung in front of my face, but I could still see Cinda upside-down, swinging higher and higher. Her hair was pulled back in a ponytail, but some strands of her glowing white hair were loose, waving freely in the breeze. The shoelaces of her soiled white sneakers were untied, and as her swinging slowed, my dizzy head confused her frown for a smile. Then it all became twisted. I spun myself up to the top of the monkey bars and watched her twisting the chains of the swing—twist and untwist—against the rules. The line of kids waiting to use the swing got wildly impatient. The one next in line shouted, "28, 29, 30, my turn!" Cinda ignored him, pushing herself off the ground with the force of her toes, up into the air. She fiercely kicked as I watched in wonder. "Ms. Rickenbacker, Ms. Rickenbacker," the line screamed in unison. Ms. Rickenbacker came running towards Cinda and asked her in a gentle voice to come down. Cinda kept spinning and spinning as the chains unwound and then swung again into the air. "Cinda, your turn is over," Ms. Rickenbacker insisted, louder this time. The swinging slowed, but Cinda twisted herself between the chains like a pretzel, shaking and screaming, kicking one foot against the other. Ms. Rickenbacker came from behind and untwisted Cinda, hugging her arms around her while the male aide grabbed her by the legs. By this time, several more kids had formed a circle around them, some giggling, others whispering into each other's ears. Me—I felt a pain in my chest as I just sat on top of the bars and didn't move. I was sure Cinda had a seizure because she missed Richard.

Even before the seasons changed and the air became cooler, Cinda hardly ever came outside anymore. Though I had given up Richard, I still peeked through the window from time to time. When she did get on her swing, she didn't swing as high. She wasn't humming or even talking to herself as she usually did. Often, she just sat there staring up at my window, waiting.

When the rains came, Mom drove me to school and picked me up. I missed playing Monkey Square. I missed Richard. All I had left was my favorite stuffed animal Monchichi. So, when I came home from school, I dragged him with me around the house. I held him next to my cheek and created a dreadful smile on my face. I would wag the monkey at Mom's face. After I did it once too many times, she yelled at me to stop, and threw Monchichi across the hallway into the mirror. When I went to pick up his drooping body from the floor, I saw my own reflection in the mirror, my noodle arms wrapped around him. I knew then that he was my only friend.

Spring came along and I walked to and from school again. Richard had disappeared, but I hadn't forgotten Monkey Square. I started it up again, even memorizing some – the first one just two squares to the left of where the safety patrol kid regularly stood wearing his red wind breaker, holding the large pole forward with the stop sign; another one on the corner where Pickard Avenue turned in to my street, Chestnut Avenue; and another in front of the two-story house painted bright pink where that old Filipino couple ran a home for the mentally disturbed.

I didn't feel too old to play Monkey Square as I now did for other games like hopscotch or Barbies, but I longed for someone to join me. I thought of Cinda—she would have loved leaping over squares—but she wasn't allowed to walk home by herself; her mom dropped her off and picked her up from school every day. The following summer, after fifth grade, Cinda and her mom moved away. I didn't know where they went.

Now that I am so many years removed from my childhood days, I don't dream of naked women nearly as much, and Richard has never returned. As for Cinda, I imagine her all grown up, still fierce, her white hair still glowing in the sunlight, wherever she is and whatever she's doing.

GIVING UP THE GHOST

You know only half the story. You know the dead haunt the living. Every story, so they say, has a beginning and an end. If this is the case, then Isobel is transfixed somewhere in between, paralyzed by grief.

She crouches in remembrance under a stream of cool water, shivering. Last night's dream: *Let go.* Or was it, *Let me go!* She had just cranked the handle from its off position to the left, expecting hot water quick. Instead, lukewarm is the best she gets. Cool, lukewarm, lukewarm, cool. She moves the handle of the color-coded faucet all the way to the halfway point between hot and cold in favor of red. *You grabbed my hand, not offered. We fell down the pit together.* The showerhead fails to spew hot water only when someone else runs hot water at the same time. But there is no one else now.

Not sure of how much time has passed since she got into the shower, Isobel shuts the water off without soaping and dries off. She drapes the towel over her back to catch the dripping water from her shower cap. *Seely, you used to say shower caps are for old ladies with curlers in their hair. Funny, Seely.*

Isobel is the sensitive, serious one. Or is it, Isobel *was* the sensitive one. Isobel is still here. Seely isn't. Isobel had been the sensitive one when compared to Seely, who is no longer here. The present and past intermingle, at least in Isobel's mind. *You used to say shower caps were for old ladies with curlers in their hair. You snickered when you said this. I could not laugh, not because it wasn't funny, but because laughing requires a kind of energy I lack.*

Her cat Tigger is scratching at the door. She can tell it is Tigger doing the scratching and not Merry because declawed cats cannot scratch like that. Even though Seely had Merry declawed long before they met, the very thought of it makes Isobel feel bitter; Isobel cannot (could not) bring herself to forgive. Mind in matters of dream and trying not to freeze. What time is it? Isobel wonders. But she won't open the door, no, not even to check the time, not even if she might be running behind. She will not open the door to let in even more cool air. She must stay warm by not running the fan, keeping the door closed, and tightening the large towel around her frail, thin body.

Isobel stands in front of the mirror. The mirror is clear. She sees herself and Seely. She stands to the farthest left of the crack she created in madness that grievous day. Seely tosses her hair back, like Cher. The long black mane still shiny and smooth despite being shampooed daily. Isobel had shared her insights gained from reading only the informative portions of fashion magazines on the best routines for healthy living. "Don't wash your hair every day; do shampoo only once or twice a week to preserve that sheen." Isobel blinks rapidly and wipes the mirror. She sees only her image in the mirror now.

Isobel had taken down all the mirrors that Seely had placed in every room except for hers. She left the one up in her bedroom because it was proffered as a gift. Seely had given her one in the shape of an oval, dismissing Isobel's rendition of Borges and mirrors: "Borges's writings repeat the symbols of labyrinths, libraries, and mirrors, among other objects. My favorite writer of all time. His stories speculate on the enigma of mirrors. He (or the other Borges, the literary one) wrote Borges & I.

They shared a love (like I do) for hourglasses and the taste of coffee. Each one of us contains multitudes."

"Whatever," Seely had said, not out of rudeness, but out of frustration that she and Isobel did not always speak the same language. She thought Isobel disliked mirrors out of superstition or fear. She misunderstood. *You thought it was silly to fear mirrors, and what is more, to imitate the thoughts and feelings of a beloved, but dead, author. I never said it was about fear. I cannot bear to see the mere reflection of an object rather than the thing itself. To see in a mirror is to see in darkness. Mirrors (or is it we?) are enigmas. Even if I had told you this, you would still shake your head and say that my resistance to mirrors is ridiculous. So much of who we are cannot be revealed through words.*

Isobel looks up at the row of eight light bulbs and squints. The fourth bulb from the left has been blinking on and off now for weeks. She will not replace it when it completely burns out. Eight bulbs are exorbitant. She will wait till seven of the eight are completely depleted and leave in just one good bulb. She turns her back to the mirror and lathers her eczema-riddled skin. The long, lighted mirror with two faucets and two sinks. *Who needs two any longer when there is just me?*

*

Seely died in a most generic fashion, from a most generic disease, as Isobel would describe it. Is it insensitive for Isobel to describe the death of her best friend this way? The only irony is that she died in the same hospital where she was born. Seely still had health coverage despite her divorce from her Navy retired husband older than her by 15 years. Famous for top-notch care, the hospital staff took good care of her until her death. As expected from cancer, all but a few sprigs of hair remained here and there. She died, as so many others do, slowly but with an array of drugs like morphine to lessen the pain and smooth the transition. First, she withdrew inward, unable to make or maintain direct eye contact with anyone. Her eyes had appeared as described by many in contact with the dying, grey and vacant. Isobel frustratingly found that she could not describe that look any other way, especially because Isobel's eyes were naturally gray. She could not get herself to say, "Seely's eyes turned grey and empty" because "empty" would sound disingenuous. "Empty" is non-descript. On the other hand, it would seem a monstrosity to stare long into eyes that appear vacant and void. Besides, the eyes of the dying wander, as if reflecting the restlessness of the dying human soul.

Then she fell into a coma. The doctors had warned this would happen. They had seen it numerous times. Then came the unnerving death rattle. Last breath. Why then does something expected, including the way a person dies, still carry an element of surprise? Isobel knew her friend was dying, for Seely's health declined rapidly once she discovered she had stage four lung cancer. *I know this is happening, I know the inevitable, but why is this happening to someone who so very much wants to live?* The trembling legs. Isobel had never read anywhere that this specific phenomenon might be part of the process. The loss of hair, yes, but Seely's answer to the question, "How old are you," to test for cognition, now that the cancer had spread. Seely said, "I'm eleven." No article on the effects of cancer, no conversation with doctors prepared for "I'm eleven" as the answer.

*

The water is rushing from the showerhead hot. Isobel takes her showers early in the morning before work for the very purpose of enjoying the hottest shower possible. Seely used to make breakfast every morning while Isobel showered. She would do the dishes too. "Not while I'm showering, I told you!" Isobel would tell Seely. "I appreciate your thoughtfulness, trying to lighten my burden." Always slow to waking. Not ready for the demands of another day.

The dermatologist had urged Isobel to shower in cool water because it is better for eczema. Store bought hair dye instructs to wash hair with cool water to preserve the color longer. Isobel defies this advice, not out of spite, but because she finds hot showers soothing. The bonus is that hot water steams the bathroom mirror that she cannot take down. She dabs moisturizer on her forehead now and spreads it over the rest of her face in circular motion. Her face appears in the fogged mirror like the blotch from Van Gogh's paintbrush, indistinct, her hair a tint of silky brown chocolate, nipples specks of pink. Clock without a face. Few spaces of visual clarity fail to guide her lotioned hands over the rest of her body. The scaly, itchy, bumpy hairline sprouting soft bristles of hair. She clumsily applies sparse amounts to the parts of her back she can reach, one hand at a time. First, she moistens each shoulder blade, then tries to reach that spot between the shoulder blades. She pauses and feels the touch of a hand not her own. At the spot just short of an itch, or a bump, possibly another big zit that has materialized overnight. Seely's fingers are rough. The ointment cools to the touch. *Like this. What would I do without you?*

The mirror is free of moisture now. And here Isobel stands alone, warm and naked. Skin dry and thirsty. *Where did I leave off?*

*

Isobel is taking a short shower because today is no shampoo hair day and because the water once again is lukewarm. In between shampoos, she uses the dry kind from an aerosol can, which Seely had pointed out contradicted Isobel's environmental concerns. Isobel drapes the towel over her back to catch water from the shower cap. The mirror is not fogged but still she lathers her body with lotion for sensitive skin not by sight but by touch. No fan on. She ignores her movements reflected in the mirror and guides her hands all over her body—face, chest and thighs, sans the ears.

In the kitchen, a boiled egg sits on the counter by the sink. Had she retrieved it from the refrigerator before jumping in the shower, to allow it to reach room temperature? Why can't she remember? You would think an errand of several succinct steps (open fridge, find Ziploc bag, close fridge, rinse egg, place on plate) would require conscious effort. But Isobel eats one boiled egg for breakfast every day; therefore, the routine makes conscious effort unnecessary. If only she had made mindfulness her daily practice as Seely had (so she claimed), then the careful, thoughtful acts of daily tasks like this would stick and prompt clarity of memory.

The dishwasher racks are drawn out. This is not the alarming thing, for Isobel has always used the dishwasher as a dish rack. So did Seely in fact; they both laughed when, through a You Tube video, they discovered that this was a common practice in Asian households of the kind they had both been raised in. What is alarming is that the dishes are warm to the touch, as if they have just been washed. Isobel pauses, reaches to open the refrigerator again, this time for the loaf of bread, but there sits one piece of toast right by the toaster, spread with peanut butter. The only thing missing is a ready-made pot of coffee. She had forgotten to prepare her daily coffee. The microwave clock blinks 6:05. She must leave by 6:45 to get to work on time. *Don't panic.* All of this has an explanation.

For the next several minutes, Isobel reflects on the state of her kitchen, but more importantly, the implications. Has she withdrawn so much into herself that she is now completely absent-minded? *The shower, the mirror, Seely and me.* She should have gone to therapy immediately, but she knows what the therapist would say. Grief happens to each person differently.

Isobel rehearses what she will say when she gets home from work several hours later today; it will be about 5:15. She prepares for what she will say to Seely, should she appear. It doesn't really matter whether the Seely that she sees is a figment of her imagination, or if the apparent contusions in her reality are manifestations of grief, guilt or a combination of things. Therapist advice she has read in the important parts of women's magazines would say: "Go with whatever transpires in the stages of grief even if you suspect they are illusions of the conscience." Call her crazy, but Isobel will thank Seely for the room temperature egg, the perfectly spread toast, and reaching the part of her back out of reach.

When Isobel steps in the front door and takes off her shoes, she notices the shoe rack is leaning to one side. Seely had reminded her to replace it. She had forgotten again. When she rises from the stool and puts on her house slippers, Seely moves toward her as natural as ever. Isobel thank Seely in words, just as she planned. Seely nods in the negative. Her mouth takes on various shapes, but no sound comes out; the air outside of her lips twirls like the smoke from a cigarette, then she sucks it in. The eyes that speak are Seely's, grey and pleading. Isobel's heart sinks right down to her cold feet.

*

Faceless face of Starry Night. Hair long and black. Seely's face. She rubs her goose-pimply skin. Hesitant to wipe the moisture from just that part of the mirror that impossibly reflects. Relieved, she sees what she expects, puffy short brown curly hair that she has come to accept. She pumps lotion into her right hand, pumping with her left. Her mirror self stays still. She waves her right hand; mirror left hand covers her crotch. She waves her hand again and her mirror head jerks simultaneously. She touches the mirror face, but the mirror does not mimic. Her mirror body collapses and so does her body.

Isobel, surprisingly, in all her knowledge of customs and culture, science and philosophy, was not aware of the various models of the superstition "break a mirror, face seven years of bad luck," when she struck the bathroom

177

mirror with the toothbrush glass the day of Seely's death. Even if she had been aware, such an irrational belief would not stop her from acting on such powerful emotion. Even though one variation says that mirrors hold the power to confiscate part of the user's soul, which might be one way to explain why sometimes she sees Seely's image in the mirror instead of her own. Or explain why the mirror fails to reflect the present reality of her actions and seems to go off on its own. Certainly, a broken mirror with the power, as the superstition goes, to trap the soul of the one who breaks it, can make that imprisoned soul behave in bizarre ways. The superstition continues: if one breaks a mirror, the bizarre mirror world traps not just one's soul, but a broken soul. Isobel has been more broken than broken since that day.

Isobel comes to. The floor feels warm. It reminds her of the trip they took together during one spring break to Seoul, Korea. She and Seely stayed two nights in a *hanok,* or traditional Korean home. The heat came from the floor. This so fascinated them both that they Googled it together at an Internet café. The traditional home uses the *ondol,* a floor-based heated rock system. Natural raw materials do not cause pollution. *You can move here to teach! We can. I'll move with you and freeload.* Isobel almost said, *like you do now.* But she bit her tongue. It was okay that Seely was only sporadically employed after her divorce. Not college educated, she had waitressed, pet sat, used her car as a taxi. Not once did she ask for money or fail to pay her share. She may not have been good at holding down a job, but she was good at saving. Oblivious to the ridiculousness of remaining crumpled on the bathroom floor, Isobel reminisces about an irretrievable past. *That's how it feels right now. Your mat next to mine. I didn't make a fuss over you invading my space. I stepped over your body to use the bathroom in the middle of the night. You did not stir at all. I used to say it was freaky how quiet a sleeper you were. Tempted to place a mirror close to your face while you were sleeping to make sure you were still breathing. Just in case.*

*

Weeks go by and the steam-less showers, ready-made breakfasts, and incomprehensible greetings at the door have nearly become a daily routine. Isobel even tried to change things by washing the dishes after dinner rather than leaving them in the sink. Still, each morning, like this, she would find her chores complete. The same death dream recurs too, as if she is now stuck in a loop of nauseating redundancy.

I used to believe that dreams are magical or the stuff of oracles, based on the fictional narratives with which I filled my mind. And then I moved on to scientific and biological explanations. Dreams are only manifestations of what happens to us in the waking day, recycling the moments of our lives in a nonlinear way. Or the revelations of previously buried feelings or passions suppressed in the unconscious mind. But then why do I feel so guilty? I felt, feel guilty both inside and outside of the dream.

Isobel wonders whether the stuff of her dream is regretful or prophetic or both.

I almost fell into a pit of infinite depth, barely hanging on to the lip. You grabbed my hand. I pleaded with you; I shouted Let go! But you held on. I wanted so badly for you

179

to let me go (to save yourself? to free me?) but you held on (infuriatingly). Then I woke up with wet eyes, still angry at your dismissal of my wishes. Did I really wish to fall into the endless pit? How did I get there? Did I fall or jump in? I don't remember, other than the feeling of being pulled down into a dark fathomless hole in the ground and liking it, you reaching your hand to grab mine. Guilt for putting you in that position of having to choose whether to "save" me? Here I go making this all about me. But isn't that what grief really is? About how the living go on?

Isobel does not yet realize, because she cannot see outside of her own experience, that all of this is about how the living *and* the dead go on.

*

Seely and Isobel stand in front of the mirror that they share. Neither of them has ever cared about taboos or proper etiquette when it comes to sharing space in preparation for the day. *You're the sister I never wanted,* Seely reminds Isobel. Isobel blinks stupidly, wiping the mirror with her hand. *Silly, it's not even fogged.* She expects Isobel to bark at her about running the hot water in the kitchen to wash the dishes left soaking in the sink all night. *Well if you had done your job at washing the dishes—it was your turn after all, I wouldn't have had to wash with hot water in the first place.* Seely looks at Isobel's dark green shower cap and laughs. One of the bulbs on Isobel's side of the mirror buzzes, the light sporadically blinking on and off. *When are you going to replace that?* she asks. She watches Isobel struggle once again to apply lotion to her back. *Here, let me help you.* She

180

squeezes just enough acne medicine on to one finger, lightly dabs the pimple and then spreads richly. The feel of the bump makes her cringe, but she doesn't say so. *What would you do without me?*

*

Isobel has gone to work. Seely sits on the love seat. Small in comparison to the larger, longer couch situated against the longer wall. Their unspoken understanding of which of the two sofas belongs to whom. Seely automatically takes her place on the smaller couch, even though Isobel's couch will be free all day. Seely likes the coziness of leaning against the arm of the love seat with her feet propped up on the opposite arm. She drapes her cat's favorite velvety-soft blanket on her legs with a book on her lap. She cannot make out the title, which appears to be written in a foreign language. She allows Merry to jump on her lap for the fact that he cannot scratch or get toenails stuck in the blanket.

She dozes off, *or something,* and the commotion of the door startles; she sees Isobel enter. She looks at the clock—5:15 on the dot. Isobel is mumbling something as she fidgets with her keys and shoes. Seely moves closer but still cannot make out the words. *Speak up* she says, *I can't understand you.* But Isobel keeps mumbling. Though Seely cannot understand the words, she senses frustration. Then Isobel collapses, as if in slow motion, as if she were folding. Seely catches her and moves her to her couch. Sitting on the edge, she rubs Isobel's feet. Eventually, Isobel opens her eyes and looks at Seely with recognition, those last pair of eyes that caught her gaze before...

Seely pinches herself and feels it. She reaches to touch

the miniature clock on the cabinet full of dolls and places it next to her ear. Hears the ticking. She remembers sequential time. *Interpret time linearly. Dreams are not bound by time. This is not all a dream after all.* She died in the recent past; The past has happened and here she is, in the present, with Isobel, where she is not supposed to be. *Let me go.* These were the last words she now remembers that she spoke. Before those last words, she could not grasp what was dream, what was hallucination or reality (her current reality at least). Once, while in a reverie of childhood, someone asked how old she was, she answered, "I'm eleven." Only when asked this question was she rudely snapped back into present time, like now, catching the troubled look in Isobel's eyes. She thinks about all she did for Isobel today and for many days now, just as she used to do before she died, how good it feels to still feel needed, but at the same time how she feels stilted somehow. She wants to transmit her thoughts, but she cannot in any ordinary human way. *I died,* she says to herself. *I really did.* She feels compelled to tell Isobel *Stop yanking me around.* So, she does. Isobel's demeanor, the whole of it, the only possible means of communication conveys utter confusion and bewilderment.

Am I still human, just a dead one? I remember, I lay dying. I feel like I am still me, my experience of my body feels the same as when I was alive, sans the physical pain. I was deathly ill, yes, I remember. Yet I still feel as I did the last moments, wanting to linger just a little longer. But also wanting to slumber some more, indefinitely. Isobel has taken the mirrors down. I don't blame her. She had her reasons for hating mirrors. She seemed to hate herself too. Yes, I remember. She still needs me, I can tell. She lets me, a ghost by all indications, touch the plagued parts of her skin that she cannot reach by herself.

*

Isobel has not always been consumed with the idea of suicide. The possibility of it, like most obsessions, as a viable escape has crept in over time. Vague feelings of torpor turned into boredom, which transformed, in broad strokes, into impossible-to-live-with anguish. Though afforded generous space, her brand of melancholy has its limits before it spreads itself into the kind of desperation that pushes one to take the plunge.

Isobel nearly did when Seely died. If Isobel could hardly stand her sense of reality (or unreality) before, the idea that she will never be able to sense the world as it really is—that reality is always filtered through our unreliable senses, then losing Seely has pushed her to the edge. Seely had been there from the day they met to make her laugh, to care for the daily tasks that sapped so much of her energy, to encourage her to look in the mirror and see what was there literally, in the moment, for what it was, without feeling the need to question its veracity. *Live in the moment as much as you can. But living in the present is impossible, for in a Borgesian way, the present is always already the past, and living mindfully is far too draining.*

Isobel is torn. As much as she has failed to let go, Seely's return stirs something troubling within her. Her glimpses of Seely leave her feeling physically exhausted, so that she catches herself collapsing often. She keeps all of this to herself, not even confiding in her parents, who had virtually adopted Seely into the family if not literally, then ceremonially. The two met in high school and stayed close even when Seely foolishly married her first boyfriend, a fellow *pinoy,* straight out of high school. After the divorce, when Seely was still in her twenties, she moved in with Isobel. Her family still in the Philippines, she spent the holidays with Seely and her family, who cooked her favorite Filipino food like lumpia and pancit, or what Seely in her teasing manner liked to call Asian spaghetti. "You're lucky to be a mutt, Isobel, really. I'm just straight up Filipino. With your exotic looks you can be very enticing, if you'd just put some effort into it." They admired each other for what the other had in the way of characteristics: "You should grow your hair into an afro, I think, Isobel. I've always wanted long straight hair I could toss like Cher, Seely." And, "Your eyes, are you sure you're not of mixed blood after all? I've never met a full-fledged Filipino with grey eyes. Let's buy wigs and colored contacts and be each other for Halloween"! Seely and her energizing way kept Isobel going. Kept her interested enough to keep on going for another day.

Isobel has thought about asking Seely's parents if they get visitations from Seely too. But she has decided against it. Besides the fact that they live far away, this feels far too personal, between just her and Seely alone. Not that she thinks post-death Seely cannot traverse vast oceans and distances. She is not sure, never has been, of what to believe when it comes to death. Seely's visits always occur at home, and always when Isobel is alone, which is almost all the time now. No boyfriend, no other friends she feels close enough to for a trial run. Maybe Seely would appear to her with others around. Maybe she won't. Isobel doesn't care to find out.

Besides the fact that she and Seely cannot communicate in any ordinary way. Isobel knows now that she is not crazy. That she in fact is being haunted by Seely or some form of her. She knows because of the literalness of the experience. The very real sensation of Seely's fingers, with which she is quite familiar. Which she has felt other than as ointment spreader. She recognizes the slightly rough texture of Seely's fingers from when they painted each other's nails. From rubbing each other's hands when they went camping overnight in the cold and forgot to bring gloves. With all her interests, she never really got caught up with ghosts before or had taken the matter too seriously beyond reading short stories with ghostly elements or watching paranormal movies from time to time. Only now that she is faced with the unnatural appearance of her supposed-to-be-dead best friend is she forced to accept their reality.

She should be excited really, for if the dead still linger in some configuration, then her wish has come true. She wished with all her power, with as much gumption as a child wishing away the monsters of the dark—*no, harder*—for Seely to survive. For wasn't it Isobel who silently wished for death? She wished for, not the pain, but the promise of disappearance so she wouldn't have to feel anything anymore. Instead, like the cruel prank of an invisible hand, Seely, the one full of life had it sucked out of her. Seely, the one who should go on thriving and living because she was so very good at it. If there is any life-truth to her dreams of late, then Isobel feels guilty for even wanting to be free of life. Her dream, her unconscious manifested its desire to ask Seely to let her go because she hoped to leave this world real soon.

Excited is not quite right. *If this ghost is really Seely, then post-cancer, post-life Seely will not let me go. I know, because Seely is still my crutch, my lifesaver. I still need you, Seely. From the time I met you, I always have.*

*

This isn't at all what she expected. Either you'd be purely an apparition, or no one could distinguish you from the living but a select few (as in "I see dead people!"). Clearly, Isobel sees her. Therefore, the effort to communicate, the constant puzzlement. Isobel was the first to think of writing messages to communicate in lieu of failed speech. She wrote on one of the whiteboards she uses for tutoring her Pre-SAT prep students, but the writing might as well have been Egyptian hieroglyphs, for Seely could not make out any of it. If it was in English as it must have been, for Isobel is no linguist or archaeologist. It is as if the wiring in Seely's mind (if she still has one) has been crossed to block cognition of written or spoken language leaving her stuck with her thoughts alone. Isobel has even drawn pictures as a last-ditch effort combined with gestures. Touching really; for all her talents, drawing is not one of them. But the drawings do not tell Seely anything she doesn't already know or remember—that Merry the male cat chases Tigger the female to bite her in the butt, still fierce and semi-feral. At least this is how Seely interpreted the two stick figures before Isobel maddeningly erased to replace with long haired stick figure: Long-haired stick figure lying down, arrow, long-haired stick figure stands. Followed by gesture of the hand pointing to Isobel's head. *I know. You can't hear me Isobel, but what I'm trying to tell you is I don't know why I'm here either. I'm just as confused as you are.*

Seely tried her post-death hand at writing too, only to be disheartened further. She cannot read, write, nor dream. Perhaps this is part of her punishment. Had she done something in life to be compelled to become a mere redundancy? Seely has grown weary. Linear time has bent into a circular web, trapping her in the consistency of repetition. She slumbers fitfully, she knows not where, suspended in a pillow of darkness without dream and wakes to find herself in the same place every morning, preparing Isobel's breakfast with no desire to partake herself. She props herself on her loveseat, rubs Merry's chin, and waits for Isobel's return fitfully. Rinse, recycle, repeat.

She tries to will herself out of here. Or will herself somewhere else, her childhood home in the Philippines, where she lived until she was five. Perhaps she fails because her memory is vague and incomplete. She envisions returning for a brief visit to her ex-husband, but that fails too. Maybe because he has a new girlfriend and the invisible hand in this puppet show looks out only for the living and cannot be troubled with the desires of the dead who've outlived their expiration date.

Seely is torn. She extends her friendship as she always did. She serves as a buffer between Isobel and her despair; but only the broken need crutches, and even Seely cannot fix what makes Isobel broken in the first place. Only Isobel can do this. Besides, Seely's life had been made rich by more than just Isobel's friendship. This loop she is caught with Isobel cannot even be called a true friendship. Not the kind of friendship they once shared. Now, whatever they have tips disproportionately in favor of Isobel's needs. *That's it. I'm here for Isobel's needs.* Isobel didn't and doesn't need Seely's writing. She doesn't need to hear a recount of Seely's dreams. Yet, maybe Seely can stop this. Stop setting out breakfast, washing the dishes, turning off the alarm clock when Isobel in her forgetfulness jumps in the shower before shutting it off. And yet...part of her still thrives in caring for the needs of others. *I'm tired, but Isobel still needs me. I see the crack in the bathroom mirror. My collection of mirrors still stowed in the closet and on the topmost kitchen shelves. She plans on putting them back up, I'm sure, in my honor. She hasn't given Merry away, something I worried she would do after I was gone. I see the way she tilts her head back teasingly the way I did with my Cher imitations, when she thinks no one sees.*

*

In the shower, Isobel tries a thought experiment. She decides she will try mindfulness, even though she used to resist; Seely insisted on the positivity of a practice the effects of which Isobel considered too shrouded in mystery. Concentrate on what is happening right this moment rather than letting your mind wander every-where else. Isobel closes her eyes under the stream of warm water.

I am still here, and I shouldn't be. I should be somewhere else. I know this because we cannot speak to each other. For all intents and purposes, we are mute. This means something. Isobel calls me here not through words but by her very demeanor, utterly melancholy and sad, unable or unwilling to let go. Let me go. Stop washing the dishes. Don't prepare breakfast. I'll let her do her own duties. I'll leave her alone.

Isobel gets herself to truly feel the flow and temperature of the water as it cascades against her skin. Subtle change to warm and warmer, now hot, just enough. Now that the water strikes just the right temperature, other thoughts distract her. *If dreams are something more than random reenactments of the moments of our lives, whether banal or special; if they are revelations of something very human, deeper than base needs, then I'd call them something other than revelations. I'd call them obscurities, inducers of mystery. It is what it is, Seely used to say. Seely, funny name. I asked when I met you, "What's your real name?" You said, with your nose scrunched and eyes narrowed, that is my real name! Not short for Priscilla? A variation on Shelly? No, don't be silly! Why can't Filipinos have interesting names other than Remedios, Teresita, or Isobel for that matter! Silly Seely. It is what it is. I am who I am. Accept the mystery and try not to read too much into it. Enjoy the moment. Back to the moment.*

*

You know how the dead haunt the living? That is only half the story. The living also haunt the dead. The living and the dead haunt each other when they refuse to let each other go. They refuse to give each other up, as if death were something to negotiate. But as it goes, every story has an end and a beginning. Just when their story was just about up, they both got stuck. Blinded by irrational guilt, need and grief, neither could see her way to the end of their story.

Once they give each other up, each can go on. Isobel, to the next stage of her life, whatever that may be. Seely, to the next realm, what the ancients have called in the most prosaic of terms (for lack of awareness or just the right words) life after death, heaven, hell, or the hereafter, maybe even everlasting sleep. Whatever the case, not bound to the middle, limbo, or the in-between of neither here nor there. Isobel only knows that the ghost of Seely has stopped haunting or helping her. Though she still misses Seely, she no longer feels utterly helpless nor the blinding grief she had felt initially, nor the guilt that plagues those who feel unjustified in continuing to live beyond the death of their loved one. She lives differently.

From time to time, of course, Isobel will think of Seely. She will see Seely, among others who have traversed her path, but not in the mirror. She will see neither clearly nor lucidly, not in the present reality. When her eyes are open, her mind sometimes wanders inward to bask in the treasure box of memory.

ARTIFICIAL MOTHER

When you try to imagine the birth, you imagine it more as a retrieval than a sudden appearance brought on by hours of maternal agony; unlike your birth and that of every other baby for thousands of generations, this one will not require hours of physical suffering. No element of surprise. Your baby will have evolved before your eyes, that is, if you visit regularly as suggested in the coming weeks.

Talk to the baby—that should be especially easy, considering the baby is suspended like a lovely seahorse for anyone to see. Don't hold back, for she can hear you. Sing to her and then watch for a response. New Birth means greater transparency. Mimic a natural pregnancy if you hope to form a bond before arrival. *Arrival. Emergence.* Which word best describes New Birth? "Arrival" and "emergence" can be used interchangeably to denote the appearance of something new. Nothing can quite compare to observing close-up and personal your baby's growth from conception to emergence; that's right—you decide that you prefer the sound of the word "emerge" and all that it connotes. Traditional mothers claimed they *felt* their baby's growth within their bellies, but you can't help but balk at that sentiment. You get to witness your baby's transformation before your very eyes. That's right, she's *your baby,* despite the distance between her body and yours.

At first, you feel a bit self-conscious, cooing and cawing and making your best baby noises, even though there is no one else in the holding room but you and her. Just behind the biobag on the wall hangs a diagram of gestation from Week 1 to Week 28. Tiny as a pea, you are relieved to see that your baby is just the right size for Week 8. The perfect artificial pregnancy. No physical discomfort, unpleasantness, or ill effects; no nausea or vomiting. No pelvic pressure, no itchy, expanding belly.

At Week 12, you play your choice of music in place of pre-recorded lullabies that mimic the human heartbeat. This set-up is well intentioned but an obvious holdover from traditional pregnancies. With neither you nor the baby possessing one, you decide that to continue playing musical rhythms like the human heartbeat would be pointless if not deceiving. Still, you agree that music is the universal language no matter the advancements, and so you play a variety with rhythms, beats and melodies conveying a range of emotions, from melancholy to elation, resignation to confusion. You play your favorite albums on the antique record player that they permitted you to set up in the private hospital room, wishing to expose your baby to the musical richness of your childhood. You are quite pleased to see signs of excitement: the baby jolts, and like a betta fish gulping underwater, her mouth rounds into an O of pure joy.

In the ensuing weeks, you play music of various eras from before the Change: Wagner's "Faust Overture"; Billie Holiday's *Essential Rare Collection;* Mariya Takeuchi's *Variety*; Keith Jarrett's *Koln Concert,* from 1975, the year your own mother was born. You close your eyes and imagine piano fingers lilting across the keys with speed and grace. Taking pleasure in exuberant bursts of "oohs" and "aahs," you lift the needle and set it down on to repeat that part, hoping the fetus will sense the joyous human energy. You and your twin got piano lessons at age six. You used to dream of becoming a solo pianist, while Sister immediately lost interest. Sister so often resisted similarity. This is how you remember it.

At one point, you think your precious baby—just look at how utterly miraculous the thing, she's yours, she's really yours! —your precious baby she looks bored, for she yawns and stretches her arms. Anything and everything she does excites you with a thrill for living that you have never felt before. Then your thrill turns into chill when you realize you cannot be certain that she is responding to the music. It could very well be the programmed simulations of a waking mother's movements, for whether naturally birthed or not, babies are often rocked to sleep this way. The baby does not need your body, and though you knew this going into it, if you still had a heart, you would have felt it drop just now. To change the mood, or rather your mood, you play something more exciting—Takeuchi's Plastic Love, the original version.

Don't hurry.
I'm sorry.
Don't worry.
I'm just playing games
I know that's plastic love
Dance to the plastic beat
Another morning comes

Remember how you got a kick out of annoying Sister by humming along to the tune, inserting words indiscriminately: I'm not in plastic love. Da-da da plastic beat, I know that morning co-o-o-o-mes. You never could be bothered to look up the actual lyrics, even though this was for you the best pop song in all the world. You were and still are fine without understanding every word, but Sister for her part found two translations of the Japanese lyrics and placed them one after another for critical analysis.

> *Don't mess up the program of love*
> *With your sudden kisses and fiery state*
> *I cleverly plan every hello and goodbye*
> *Because everything comes to an end*
> *Don't hurry!*
>
> *Despite my sudden kisses and passionate looks*
> *Don't get upset with the program of this love*
> *I've been dealt with hellos and goodbye's so neatly*
> *In due time, everything will end—Don't hurry!*

Comparing the two versions, Sister insisted that the switching of the first two lines is of important significance. "Trivial you say?" she said in her slow, matter-of-fact tone. "I think not. The first version emphasizes that "you" not mess up love with your lustful actions, whereas in the second, the speaker places responsibility on herself for failing to inhibit her passion. The actor of the first version, then, is "you," whereas the actor of the second is the speaker, "I" signified by "my." Sister approached every-thing in life with her penchant for literary analysis, which always irritated you. Unlike you, she could not seem to compartmentalize. You both possessed a keen intellect, consistently performed at the highest level, top of your class, but you saw her inability to acclimate to changing circumstances as a character flaw. "Lighten up," you told her, "Which translation accurately describes the songwriter's intentions? Well, I don't care all that much."

Hoping to one-up your twin, you rolled your eyes. "The

gist," you insisted, "is this: 'Don't hurry me up to fall in love because I've been hurt so badly.' It doesn't really matter who said what. Get to the big picture, to the heart of it straight away. If you really want to get technical (and just then, you had to work hard to suppress your impatience), the phrases 'program of love' and 'plastic love' both connote a sense of the fake. The speaker has learned her lesson; she wishes for love as an automatic performance, as cold and distant as she has become."

You don't stop there. You're on a roll:

Every guy that asks me out ironically looks just like him

For some reason my memories run wild

"She must have fell fast and hard for 'him' in the heat of passion, and just as hard and fast, the romance crashed and burned. Her memories of him have made her cautious.

Don't hurry, don't make the same mistake, besides

Never take loving someone like me serious
Love is just a game, I just want to have fun

"Very good, very good!" Sister mocked. "See, if you take the time to break things down, then you can understand anything!"

With her coaxing, you just participated with Sister in sucking the life out of your favorite song. Music, like all art is highly subjective, and what this song means for you won't be the same as what it means for others. What does it mean to you, Baby? you say, returning to the present.

Your Baby's eyes are closed. Caught up in a reverie of memories, you forgot to observe her reactions. But that's okay. This isn't the last time you will play one or another version of Plastic Love.

On your next visit, you post clever quotes about motherhood all over the plain white walls to help keep your spirits up:

"[Motherhood is] the biggest gamble in the world. It is the glorious life force. It's huge and scary—it's an act of infinite optimism."—Gilda Radner

"When you are a mother, you are never really alone in your thoughts. A mother always has to think twice, once for herself and once for her child." —Sophia Loren

You find the latter especially relevant, holding up despite having been articulated so many decades ago. You haven't been a mother for very long, but like a long-distance lover, your thoughts are consumed with your prospective descendent and you long for the moments when you can be together.

You wait until Week 16 to speak intelligible human language. Early language development still begins before birth as far as you know, and as with music, babies remember certain sounds such as vowels from their mother's language. Hi there, baby. How are you? You over there, me over here. Even with the reassurance that the baby can hear and react to all sounds—inside and out—you can't help but think it all pointless; for even if the child may someday remember it, speaking as a way of communicating will soon be rendered obsolete by the ability of Trans-humans to communicate wirelessly.

Within you, an internal battle ensues. The more you speak to the baby, the more impatient you become. Just like the restlessness of your younger days. Only now, it feels visceral, physiological. Your tongue cannot keep up with the rush of thoughts and memories. So you spew un-sentences instead: *When Tommy met Annabelle gale storm umbrella. Sister marathon sweat breath* and feel guilty all the more. Does it really matter whether you speak in complete sentences or in fragments? The point of talking to the baby—*your baby*—is to soothe it by the sound of your voice, isn't it? The way that the sound of music soothes whether the words make any sense? Yet, you find yourself wanting to slow down and enunciate each word, as Sister used to do. With her propensity for details, Sister was more like Father and his skill of storytelling.

Frustrated by the things you can no longer say, you think to write instead. That's it. You will write in the hospital room and in your bedroom. The hand has the strength of bone and muscle, doesn't it? Whereas the tongue is soft and weak. Tame your impatient mind by the force of a strong hand. Wouldn't typing be faster? Yes, but as you find with your first penned pages, there is nothing like the sensation of the hand gliding swiftly across paper like that of a pianist, nothing like the thrill of the hand-writer's high. From then on, with just three months left, you keep a journal of your thoughts addressed to the Un-Emerged.

*

Week 17. I would be feeling signs of the quickening by now. Like Mother. Look! she said to Father, look one them is kicking! He felt the kick on the palm of his hand just then and relished the moment. Will you be kicking soon?

Dearest, should I tell you a story about me and EM? By the time you read this, you already know your roots. You know that you originated unconventionally, untraditionally my skin and from his nanobot sperm. Writing that just now reminds me of just how unreal all of this still seems. Maybe EM has told you his story. More likely he hasn't had to. You can communicate from one brain to another instantly, so why wouldn't you? As for me, you may have already plugged in, and so you will have perceived that we shared a close kinship, have sensed the wide bandwidth of pleasant emotions. When I had to choose, I chose him and he was all in. I will no longer linger in this narrative. Rather, I will tell you the story of your grandparents, two very special biological human beings whom you sadly, will never meet.

There was nothing extraordinary about the night that Val met Annabelle in Swansea, Wales. Caught in her very first gale storm, Annabelle sprung open her umbrella, useless against the powerful winds. She held the inside-out umbrella over their heads as they ran into the campus flat together. It was the small things that moved him: her upturned nose, the glow about her as she tripped over the threshold. Later in the haven of his dorm room, he wept neither tears of joy nor of sadness, but an array of emotions combined. So caught up in the reverie of her, he had not even noticed the seconds slip into minutes, the way I imagine time for you bears no significance. There he sat soaked down to his skin, anticipating when they might meet again.

Anabelle, on the other hand, had not thought much of their meeting; in fact, for her it was neither chance nor fate that brought them together, but a sort of good-natured defiance. The wind gusts would not get the better of her, just as no challenge ever had. Don't tell your father, she said. It took me awhile to warm up. After all, your father was like me just an American. Truly, I expected to meet someone more exotic during my study abroad. It was his consistent efforts to win me over that won me over, she said, in her abridged version.

Father had been hyper-sensitive. The opposite of Mother, who couldn't be bothered with the time and energy it took to attend to intensity of feeling. He told— *not just any story*—but those uniquely his. He narrated with such vividness and feeling that brought his story alive in my mind's eye. He story-told to both me and Sister, your aunt, who would have passed Father's stories down to her own children just as I am doing now, had she survived. It hurts my hand, for I have never written this fast before; but I command, the biological part that refuses to give ground to the nanobots that infiltrate my mind and expand it exponentially.

Week 20. Sorry to wake you. I've learned that in my absence you started to sleep and wake on regular cycles. It has been three weeks. I took a "baby moon." Silly right? It's not like I've done anything particularly strenuous or stressful with this "pregnancy." But again, in imitation of a traditional one and as one last hurrah before...I'm sorry. I didn't do any "baby" things, such as getting your baby room ready. I didn't even go out of town. I stayed in mostly, occasionally venturing out to the Virtual Theater. I can't seem to stay away from those few public venues that remind me of Mother Father Sister. Though they've changed drastically, the old movie house bars and eateries-turned virtual reality domes preserve remnants of the past. Thanks to the few left like me who've retained biological human-ness, posters of 20th century classics like *Planet of the Apes, Star Wars,* and early 21st century ones like *Blade Runner 2040* still ornament the walls.

I'm supposed to be feeling pretty good at this point because the risk for miscarriage or premature labor would have passed by now. In lieu of a natural pregnancy, how do I feel? I miss you when we are apart. I am sorry you don't get the advantage of proximity, to respond to a hand rubbing the belly, or to be lulled to sleep from Mother's activity. But the advantage is that negative feelings, like the blues, do not directly impact you. With you inside that biobag and me outside, we are forced to bond from a remove. Of course, that doesn't mean we cannot bond at all. Trading one kind of blindness for another, or if you like, the heightening of one sense over another. I can't feel you, but I can see you with my own eyes.

Your intelligence will surpass even EM's—certainly mine. He chose a total mind upload, and soon, his mind will interface with yours. Call it foolish, but I wanted to retain what I could of this biological body, though limited and cumbersome by comparison to the new and improved 2 and 3.0's. Oh, there I go, writing about EM and me again, even though I said that I wouldn't. There is so much you will learn, quickly and effortlessly, when you emerge.

Your skin is wrinkled and transparent, like the skin of someone who has sat in the bath too long. You may or may not get to experience the unique conditions of having human skin for long; it depends on your choice of embodiment. Your hair appears feathery and fine, the color of dark chocolate like mine. What have you, or will you inherit from EM? First, his intellect. Second, genes completely free of disease. As for physical traits, I cannot say, for EM is constantly altering his physical manifestation, his embodiment. He loves the plasticity.

Plastic Love. I love that song so much. Exactly how many times I've listened I cannot recount, but it replays in my mind randomly, different lines at different times. Oh— listen to the haunting sounds of almost every song on the album. You don't need to understand the language to be moved. Before Sister forced translation on me, I was transfixed by the entirety, like standing from a distance and absorbing the whole of a painting, as opposed to standing close and examining each brush stroke. Hard to explain in words what in a song moves one. Sister was not as inspired; for her, the literal meaning of the words overpowered the aesthetic effect of musical melody. For her, such talk of love and broken hearts was too prosaic. Not that she did not enjoy music. If she did, she didn't say. I can only go by memory, which is lucid now and pristine. Oh, the thrill of it, to suddenly remember all the things connected to those I love the most, like waking up remembering all last night's dream.

Just to annoy Sister, I amped up the volume of *Plastic Love* even more, just like I'm doing now. I want to make sure the music breaks through the barrier of the plastic bag where you reside. *Plastic love. Plastic love.*

*

I just re-watched the classic *Being John Malkovich*, the premise being much like experience-beaming. I haven't tried it myself, for I find no need. I relish my memories of real-life connection to those closest to me. I'm sure you will relish experience-beaming the way kids in my day were addicted to video games. I can't say I can blame you. To literally have access to anyone's sensory experience, including mine. You will be so addicted to the phenomena, virtually realizing what it's like to be someone. To make up for the absence of a real childhood, you will spend your credits on Parent-Child Adventures at Disneyland, Disneyworld, all the now nearly extinct theme parks. Just saying this now sends chills through me. You'll be able to experience that feeling too, artificially.

Week 21. Valencia, born 1969, had a twin named Lulu. They were born the year the first humans walked on the moon. Before the Internet, smart phones, and virtual reality video games, they had the outdoors to explore— Indian clay, marbles, and tadpoles. For the 5th grade book float contest, they re-created a scene from Winnie the Pooh and won first place. Lulu molded and baked figures out of playdough. Val found the shoebox and cut out construction paper. Lulu designed the float but shared the prize money with her twin brother anyway, a whole five dollars which bought them a Beverly Cleary book, stickers, and a Mad Lib based on their favorite Saturday morning cartoon, *Scooby Doo.* Aunt Lulu lived with us after her husband died. Within a year of Father's death, she died too. Not surprising for siblings as close as those two. Theo Van Gogh died six months after Vincent Van Gogh, my favorite artist of all time. Though the cause of death was said to be syphilis, more likely he died inconsolable, separated forever from the one closest to his heart.

Why did I choose to have a child now, so much later in life? On the other end of the spectrum, why not wait? With the prospect of eternity, time ought to be a luxury and endeavors ought to lose their sense of urgency. Yet, as an In-Between, I felt more than ever that it was either now or never to finally have a child of my own. Maybe because it is still hard for me to believe one can live a life without fear of sickness or death. Mother died at 50, Father at my age, 55, and sister at 30, not long before biotechnology triumphed over the deadliest diseases. I lived the first few decades of my life pre-Singularity, lived to see those closest to me die premature deaths. Shock turned into anger, then anger into grief, grief into fear, which led to the decision of a hysterectomy. Mother died of uterine cancer. I was told I had a 50/50 chance getting the same cancer, I did not want to gamble on my life. I had always wanted a child, but I told myself I could adopt. This was when cancer was still the number one killer. How was I to know the cure was just around the corner?

I tried to ease the loss by adopting pets. But I felt something was still missing. A friend told me that as much as she loved her kitties, it could not come close to the sensation of having her own baby. Though by artificial means—you are still my offspring. I almost couldn't believe it possible, but here you are, developing before my eyes.

When I had my womb removed, I thought I had lost my chance to conceive permanently. But just when I thought I'd made peace with it... here we are. I didn't deserve it, but I got a second chance.

Oh, dear *Amelia, Annabelle, Simone, or Veronica*—you decide, for one name cannot encompass all that you are or all that you will be. Sadness engulfs the most of me, having nothing of course to do with you, but all to do with the past. Why them, not me? I smoked, while Sister never did. Yet she was the one who died of lung cancer. Started in her lungs and spread like wildfire to her brain. If only she had lived to see—she could have had her mind freed from the brain consumed with disease and uploaded to another substrate. That's what EM did; he chose Body 3.0, not because of the threat of disease, but because of its plasticity. *Plastic love.* Not only is my memory precise and pristine, so is my ability now to predict with certainty; based on where we have been, I know where we are going.

*

[Circa 2060, Age 5]

You are precocious. No public schooling, for all you need is available through inter-neuronal connection. In your wisdom, you will have chosen to outweigh your biological characteristics with the nonbiological so that the latter will outweigh the former. You'd rather interface with the Interconnected Mesh rather than bother with face-to-face contact.

[Age 20]

You are a completely software-based human now, for why wouldn't you be? With nonbiological intelligence billions of times more powerful, and with the essential promise of immortality, why wouldn't you? The Singularitarians have argued all along that nonbiological intelligence is still human, derived from a combination of human and machine civilization. Is software-based human an accurate description?

[Circa Pre-and Post-Birth]

When you emerge, you won't need Mother's milk; all the better since I have none to give. You'll learn to walk very early on. Between Sister and me, she was the late bloomer. I learned to walk at two, while she did at three. I got my period at 13, she at 14. Late to life milestones, early to death. Started getting headaches every day and slept most hours of the day until sleep became permanent. Just two years after her death, they found the cure to cancer. I tried to console myself that the naysayers are right, that with death no longer a threat, life has lost some meaning, if not all. How can you appreciate life without its opposite? How can there be positive without negative, yin without yang, darkness without light. You need contraries, opposites to make complete. None of this is consoling, for I still miss Sister Father Mother. Especially Sister, bone of my bone, flesh of my flesh.

You'll have no reason to bask in memory, to respond with feeling. For even if I chose to live eternally, you and I—this parent-child relationship—will have become obsolete. Already as I speak, Mother is unnecessary for you to thrive. If any biological humans are left, they may or may not be the storytelling animals they once were. If they are, they prefer the storytelling power of virtual reality. Already you have grown impatient with slow, language-based communication. My storytelling, primitive by comparison.

I have sent out the entire flow of my sensory experience onto the Web that you can access by simply plugging in virtually. So why bother leaving you this diary? Why when you can think and feel all I've thought and felt instantaneously? Because I need you to know the story of your ancestry, the stories of those you'll never get to plug into—Mother, Father, Sister. I wish I wish for you to learn and understand your heritage in the manner of a biological human. Consider experience beams as supplementary to the richness of first-person connection. For true, some things cannot be expressed with words. But do this for me and for Mother Father and Sister's memory, as you read please, close your eyes and form images in your mind, rather than having them formed for you. Like the superior sound of a vinyl record, this is the real thing. I tell you stories from the heart I once had. I hope my stories touch you to the soul as Mother's and Father's touched mine.

Since I can remember, Sister looked for ways to make herself different. When I grew my hair out, she cut hers every month. When we shopped for clothes, she said, "You choose first," then when I picked out multi-colored attire, she ran to the black rack. One thing she could not forego even if she tried was our shared love for running, addiction to the runner's high. We trained together for our first triathlon and finished at the same time, hands on thighs, flushed faces, sweat pouring down our faces, panting. She felt my heartbeat and I felt hers. Our hearts beat rapidly, eyes fluttered, then we embraced.

As she lay dying, she said, "No more pain, no more pain," I held her right hand and pumped the Morphine with every moan from pain. Consoling me rather than the other way around, as she had in her own way when we were children, when I feared death more than anything. Disenchanted with magical thinking, I came to understand quite early that the reason Road Runner kept returning even after falling off a cliff repeatedly was because cartoons were moveable drawings. When our bunny froze to death in a rainstorm after we forgot her in the backyard, I knew she wasn't coming back. Sister made a stuffed snake and gave it as a gift offering, taking the blame. Never mind that I was not fond of snakes. It was her way of saying it was going to be okay.

Her heartbeat slowed as mine raced. Each beat like a tiny hammer in my chest. Sometimes I still feel for a pulse when caught up in memory. I should have lay dying too, should have felt my heart slow to a stop in perfect synchrony with hers. Now I have no heart, but I still have my breath. I chose to keep my lungs. I had been a coward by having my heart removed, but I would not let them touch my lungs, no. I would keep the lungs in tribute to Sister, and maybe, just maybe, I would get what I deserve.

*

Baby girl, if you've placed me deep, deep, in your mind file, how often, if ever, do I emerge in memory? Does the thought of me make you feel sad, angry, or a combination of feelings? Do you then choose to file me back, far back, and like a dream that quickly fades upon waking—will I fade away for you? Will you still be able to dream even though you will no longer need sleep? Do you dream? If not, plug in. Connect to a dream of a dream. I will be frank, no hiding anything from you, for all this I am writing right now is not part of the flow of experiences I already sent into the worldwide archive. For true, I desire death, and desire—if it is unfulfilled—is a form of dream—elusive, just out of reach.

Oh beloved, if you are reading my words, then I have

not burned my diary as I was often wont to do. Optimism won over pessimism and through the fog of doubt, I see a spark of me in you, just a glimpse. I chose calendar time, limitation, the Old-World Ways, Death as a way of Life. Whatever form you have chosen, you have, you will, thrive. I know this. I know the world had to change; I just couldn't change with it.

> *I' m just playing games*
> *I know that's plastic love*
> *Dance to the plastic beat*
> *Another morning comes*
> *Because everything comes to an end*

Don't hurry! Mind racing. Story slipping slipping. Never pregnant. Anticipation. Nesting instinct *I'm sorry* never kicked in. Should have baby-proofed room for You. *I'm sorry.* Ought to have cleared out clutter: letters, photos, greeting cards. Concert tickets, sheet music, drawings and doodles. For you. This shirt salvaged like so many things from the good years. Soon forge immortal clothes replace any and all reminders of fragility, mortality. Words like these immortal too, emblazoned in your perfect memory. *Play play play beat beat beat beat I'm just playing games I'm not I'm not playing games playing play play play I know that's plastic I I know I know that's plastic love -tic love -tic love What is Mother? Don't mess up You I Don't worry Mother instructs. Plas-tic lo-o-o-o-ve. Never take loving someone like me seriously Love is just a game* Mother Woman of few words. *Woman cold as ice.* Words— heavy, burdensome. Dreams remembered in fragments. Wake half cognizant of dreams. Will you, do you dream?

Another morning *co-o-o-mes.*

Touch of a hand *plastic* brushed against brow and cheek plastic sitting by fire lilt of voice sight unfiltered without crutch of *plastic* technology *plastic* through veil of transformation— *plastic*—I see you in me.

Acknowledgements

Some pieces in this collection originally appeared in the following publications:

Big Bridge Magazine: "Backwards"
Big Bridge Magazine: "God is in the Ceiling"
Big Bridge Magazine: "Watch Out for Highway Workers"
Crack the Spine: "Giving Up the Ghost"
Eclectica Magazine: "Death—A Play"
Erotoplasty: "Waking Hours"
Fearsome Fascinations Anthology: "Schemas"
Fleas on the Dog: "Artificial Mother"
Hobart Pulp: "Not this Town"
The Latent Print: "Monkey Square"
Luna Luna Magazine: "Dream Reality"
Luna Luna Magazine: "On Death, Dreams, and Memory"
The New Urge Reader 2: Erotic Fiction by New Women Writers: "NonTouch"
Pleiades: "Day of No Dead"
Quickly: "After-Image"
Stirring: A Literary Collection, Vol 15, Ed. 9: "One Photo of Miguel Cecilio"
Uppagus: "The thing about bruises is that they heal."
wordriver: "Arms and Hands"

About Atmosphere Press

Atmosphere Press is an independent, full-service publisher for excellent books in all genres and for all audiences. Learn more about what we do at atmospherepress.com.

We encourage you to check out some of Atmosphere's latest releases, which are available at Amazon.com and via order from your local bookstore:

Buildings Without Murders, a novel by Dan Gutstein
Peaceful Meridian: Sailing into War, Protesting at Home, nonfiction by David Rogers Jr.
SEED: A Jack and Lake Creek Book, a novel by Chris S McGee
Rags to Rags, nonfiction by Ellie Guzman
Shining in Infinity, a novel by Charles McIntyre
Southern. Gay. Teacher., nonfiction by Randy Fair
Willie Knows Who Done It, fiction and poetry by Hans Krichels
Last Dance, short stories by Nicole Zelniker
The Fleeing Company, a novel by Kyle McCurry
The Testament, a novel by S. Lee Glick
On a Lark, a novel by Sandra Fox Murphy
Ivory Tower, a novel by Grant Matthew Jenkins
Tailgater, short stories by Graham Guest

About the Author

Tina V. Cabrera currently resides in the ATX area with her husband, dog, and two cats. She teaches as Assistant Professor of English for Temple College and devotes her free time to writing and making art. Visit her website at tvcannyuncanny.com.